1

2

3

4

## Key to front cover pictures

*1. The Llanberis Lake Railway with the Snowdon range in the background.*
*2. The Earl of Merioneth on the Ffestiniog Railway.*
*3. Snowdon from the Pyg track.*
*4. Caernarfon Castle.*

# Exploring Snowdonia by Rail and Foot

by

**Guy Williams**

Published by Leading Edge Press & Publishing Ltd.,
The Old Chapel, Burtersett, North Yorkshire, DL8 3PB.
☎ (0969) 667566

ISBN 0-948135-23-9

A CIP Catalogue record for this book is available from the British
Library.

Edited by Barbara Allen
Series Editor: Stan Abbott
Sketch maps by Nicholas Bagguley*
Design and Type by Leading Edge Press & Publishing Ltd.
Colour reprographics by Impression, Leeds
Printed and bound in Great Britain by Ebenezer Baylis and Son Ltd.,
Worcester

* The maps which accompany the walks in this book are for guidance only.
The publishers strongly recommend that walkers also carry the relevant
Ordnance Survey sheet. The appropriate maps for the areas covered are:
Landranger series — Sheets 115, 116, 124, 125 and 135; Outdoor Leisure
series — Sheets 16, 17, 18 and 23.

# Foreword

I am pleased, on behalf of the Snowdonia National Park Authority, to be given the opportunity to commend the experience of Snowdonia that this book presents. It offers guidance on how the various wildlife walks, landscapes, wildlife and views of the park can be enjoyed to the full without adding to the congestion, noise and pollution which come with the motor car.

Whilst rail and foot exploration relieves the Park from the worst effects of the motor car, it also allows the individual to enjoy its splendours without the frustration of traffic congestion, finding parking spaces and hazardous country lanes.

Using public transport — a combination of British Rail services, narrow gauge railways and local buses — means more freedom to enjoy Snowdonia whilst minimising the pressures on the park itself.

The Snowdonia National Park Authority is a strong supporter of Gwynedd's public transport network and has used it to initiate the Snowdon Sherpa Bus Service. This is a useful circular bus service which allows walkers to explore Snowdon's many footpaths, unrestricted by the area's innate parking problems. I commend the experience of Snowdonia by rail and foot and hope that many readers will try this.

A little careful planning and preparation will reward the visitor with a relaxed and satisfying experience of Snowdonia at its best.

Alan Jones,
*National Park Officer*

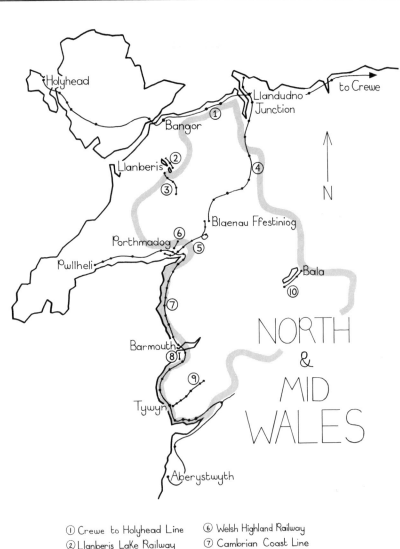

NORTH
&
MID
WALES

① Crewe to Holyhead Line
② Llanberis Lake Railway
③ Snowdon Mountain Railway
④ Conwy Valley Line
⑤ Ffestiniog Railway
⑥ Welsh Highland Railway
⑦ Cambrian Coast Line
⑧ Fairbourne and Barmouth Railway
⑨ Talyllyn Railway
⑩ Bala Lake Railway

Snowdonia National Park Boundary

# Contents

# Acknowledgements

The publisher would like to thank the Snowdonia National Park Authority for its assistance with the production of this book, in particular Marian Rees for reading the manuscript.

Thanks are also due to all the staff of the many railways featured in the forthcoming pages who have kindly supplied information and photographs.

# Author's note

As far back as the 17th Century, and probably even before that, my male ancestors on my father's side — my grandfather (Taid), my great-grandfather, my great-great-grandfather, and so on — earned their living by farming in various parts of Snowdonia. This book covers, in every sense of the words, familiar ground.

In spite of the affinity I feel, deep in my bones, with the soil and rock of Snowdonia, I cannot spell with certainty all the local place names. So many different versions exist, both in Welsh and English, on signposts and in books and on maps, ancient and modern. Conway has become 'Conwy' in my lifetime, and Caernarvon 'Caernarfon'. Dolgelley is now usually spelled 'Dolgellau', though my father used to teach us children the engaging slander:

"If ever you go to Dolgelley,
Don't stay at the Lion Hotel.
There's nothing to put in your belly,
And no one to answer the bell..."

In this book, I have taken orthographical advice, when in doubt, from the relevant Ordnance Survey 'Outdoor Leisure' maps ( *see page 4).*

I have to thank a number of people for the help they have given me whilst I have been writing this book. I am especially grateful to Mr D W Allan of the Welsh Highland Railway; Mrs A Connell, Gwydir Castle, Llanrwst; Mrs Duncalf, Ro Wen; Mr Norman Gurley, Marketing Assistant, the Ffestiniog Railway; Mr R J Hailes, the Talyllyn Railway; Mr Roy Hardiman, Manager, Rheilffordd Llyn Tegid, the Bala Lake Railway; Mrs Jones, Talsarnau; Mr Nigel Markham, the Fairbourne & Barmouth Steam Railway; Mrs Gweniona Pugh, Abergynolwyn; Miss Marian Rees, National Parks Office, Penrhyndeudraeth; Mr and Mrs John Roberts, Ro Wen; Mr D Rogerson, General Manager, the Snowdon Mountain Railway; Dr Glyn Thomas, Gwydir Castle, Llanrwst; Mr D Woodhouse, Manager, the Talyllyn Railway; Mr Bruce Yarborough, Commercial Manager, the Llanberis Lake Railway; and many other kind friends.

Finally, I would advise walkers to wear strong footwear, and to carry waterproof clothing and provisions. The maps mentioned above are recommended, and so is a compass. Where ever you are, please observe the Country Code!

# Snowdonia's unique attractions

In 1947, the British Government decided to establish the country's first National Parks. The committee appointed to do this recommended that Snowdonia should be among the first to be created. This was not surprising, for Snowdonia is a dramatically beautiful region that culminates in Yr Wyddfa, at 3,560 ft the highest mountain peak in England and Wales. This book will help you to explore Snowdonia.

When the members of the committee started to define the boundaries of the Snowdonia National Park, they found that they had to look outside the world-famous cluster of peaks. There were districts that had not been previously regarded as parts of Snowdonia, but were too good to be left out of the North Wales National Park. The Committee's wider interpretation of the word 'Snowdonia' will be followed in this book.

It is, however, the mountains of Snowdonia that have first claim on the visitor's attention. Their extraordinary rock formations, caused by volcanic action and by erosion as well as by the stresses and strains of more than one Ice Age, attract and impress the ordinary holiday-maker, as well as the professional geologist. And they are accessible. The most spectacular parts of the great Lliwedd-Yr Wyddfa-Crib Goch horseshoe (for example) can be approached on foot, though experienced climbers only should leave the established paths.

The steep up-and-down, highland-and-valley nature of the greater part of Snowdonia has largely determined the way in which most of the people of these parts have lived during the past two or three thousand years. Unlike the English, who learned under the manorial system to live in small settled communities, the herdsmen and flock keepers of Snowdonia have had to set up self-contained isolated homesteads, with each family living away from all others on its own pastures. Many of the lonely farms in Snowdonia stand on sites chosen for habitation before the Romans landed in Britain.

Protected by this isolation, and in defiance of foreign infiltration, the people of Snowdonia have been able to preserve in a remarkable way the ancient British, or 'Brythonic', culture and in the form of the Welsh language, which is one of the oldest living languages

*Left: Clogwyn du'r Arddu, beneath Snowdon summit. (Jim Perrin)*

in Europe. Here are just a few of the words that recur most frequently in Welsh place names. You can look out for them as you explore Snowdonia. In many instances they will draw your attention to some point of local interest, or to a noteworthy geographical feature:

**Aber**: A place where a river enters the sea, or a larger river
**Afon**: A stream or river
**Bach** (or **Fach**): Small
**Bedd**: A grave
**Bwlch**: A gap between mountains; a pass
**Caer**: A castle or military camp
**Cantref**: An ancient division of land
**Capel** (or **Gapel**): A chapel
**Castell**: A castle or stronghold
**Coed**: A wood or thicket
**Cwm**: A valley or hollow
**Eglwys**: A church
**Ffynnon**: A well or spring
**Gwern** (or **Wern**): A wet area with alders
**Llan**: A church or sacred enclosure
**Mawr**: Great or large
**Moel** (or **Foel**): A bare hill
**Mynydd** (or **Fynydd**): A mountain
**Neuadd**: A hall
**Plas**: A large house or hall
**Pont** (or **Bont**): A bridge
**Rhos**: An open moor
**Rhyd**: A ford
**Sarn**: A causeway
**Tre, Tref** or **Dre**: A home or hamlet
**Tyddyn**: A farmstead or small holding
**Uchaf**: Higher or highest
**Ynys**: An island

These colours may help you to identify particular places:
**Coch** (or **Goch**): Red
**Du**: Black
**Glas**: Blue (if water) or green (of fields)
**Gwyn** (or **Wyn**): White
**Melyn**: Yellow
**Rhudd**: Reddish

Pwll du would be 'a black pool' — perhaps one of the dark wells in which mysterious creatures were commonly believed to survive.

The relative loneliness of Snowdonia has made it a rewarding area for the keen bird watcher to explore. In AD 1188, Giraldus Cambrensis (Gerald the Welshman) wrote of:

"...The mountains called by the Welsh 'Eryri', but by the English 'Snowdon' or 'Mountains of Snow'..."

'Eryri' in the ancient British language meant 'a breeding place of eagles'. No bird watcher is likely to see golden eagles in Snowdonia today, but among the larger species to be encountered are buzzards, carrion crows, choughs, peregrine falcons, ravens and red and black grouse. The more interesting smaller birds to be seen in Snowdonia include the dipper, the goldcrest, the grey wagtail, the kingfisher, the meadow pipit, the ring ousel, the wheatear and the wren. The rare red kite has also been reported.

Botanists too enjoy exploring Snowdonia. They concentrate, usually, on the Glyder and Snowdon cliffs, where the character of the rocks and the adequate supplies of water ensure a luxuriant flora. One gully above Llyn Idwal is actually known as "The Hanging Gardens". There are safer places to explore nearer sea level, where the dunes harbour many rare species.

Whatever your interests, exploring Snowdonia will provide you with excitement and pleasure. This will apply however you travel. Approaching this spectacular region by rail and on foot is to be particularly recommended though, and for a very good reason — for much of your time, you will be able to regulate your own speed. You will be able to halt when you like, and for as long as you wish. As that great Welshman W H Davies asked:

"What is this life, if full of care,
We have not time to stand and stare?"

Other forms of transport may have their advantages, but they also have their drawbacks. A motor car may take you quickly and easily to the top of a celebrated pass, but it can also tempt you, during the summer months, into narrow lanes that were never intended for heavy holiday traffic. In July and August some roads in Snowdonia are now almost as congested as busy city streets. Hardly relaxing! This book suggests an alternative, more refreshing, way of exploring Britain's second largest National Park.

# The wealth of Snowdonia

If you are exploring Snowdonia for the first time, you may get the impression that much of the high ground is a barren, rocky waste. This is far from being true.

The Romans were astute exploiters of the lands they conquered and in Snowdonia they mined copper, lead and, possibly, gold ores. Probably, they took over workings that were already old when they arrived on the scene. Some Snowdonian slate mines still provide employment for local men — although they no longer, like their predecessors, have to stay in barrack accommodation high up on the bleak mountains during the working week. Many of the ruins of these buildings may still be visited.

Slate quarrying was a major industry for over 100 years. The great quarries once teemed with life and activity as massive chunks of mountainside were converted into reliable roofing materials that were carried by rail all over Britain, and shipped most profitably to distant parts of the world. Now, most of the quarries are disused although some still produce slates, as well as attract visitors.

The traditional methods of the Welsh slate workers can be studied today at Gloddfa Ganol Slate Mine and Llechwedd Slate Caverns, Blaenau Ffestiniog and at the Welsh Slate Museum close to the Lake station of the Llanberis Lake Railway ('Rheilffordd Llyn Padarn'). Visitors can see how, with a wonderfully sure touch, a craftsman would split a bulky slab of rock into sheets of exactly the required thickness. The slates would then be divided into various categories according to their size. The largest were known as 'Queens'. The smaller grades were classified as 'Duchesses', 'Countesses' and 'Ladies', in descending order of magnitude.

Wherever you go in Snowdonia you will see sheep — wild goats, too, in some isolated places. Welsh rural communities in Snowdonia depend on sheep farming. It is their living and their way of life. So please keep your dogs under very, very strict control, preferably on a lead, when on the hills.

Welsh mountain sheep can survive outdoors under extremely hard conditions. A good proportion of them live out on the wild high ranges throughout the year, whatever the weather, nourishing themselves on wiry stunted grasses, and not much else. But, of course, there is much shepherding to be done, and the movement of flocks from high to low ground, and vice versa, according to the season. Through many generations of hard living, the native sheep have developed characteristics that make them more suitable than other breeds of sheep for withstanding the rigours of the climate. The Welsh mountain sheep's fleece is especially wiry and water-resistant, for instance. A peculiarity of a mountain sheep is its 'cynefin', a particular patch on the mountain to which it will return each summer with its new lamb. The lamb, in its turn, will adopt the same 'cynefin'.

On all but the very highest slopes of the mountains of Snowdonia, you will see enclosed areas (in Welsh, ffriddoed) bounded by high drystone walls. These walls were primarily intended to separate the various owners' sheepwalks; others were field boundaries.

The building of every mile of wall needed hundreds of hours of hard, back-breaking toil. Many of the stones used were dug out of the land and gathered to form boulder-free slopes and fields which could then be ploughed.

During this century, other enterprises have thrived in Snowdonia. The work of the Forestry Commission has been vastly extended, for instance, though the Commission's fondness for conifers has not always won unanimous approval; now, some of their plantations are being transformed into interesting Forest Parks. And there are the various organisations that encourage such leisure-time activities as rock-climbing, canoeing, pony trekking and hang gliding. Fastest growing of all, however, has been the tourist industry, founded on the genuine, warm-hearted hospitality that has always been associated with the Welsh. 'Croeso i Gymru', say the signposts as you enter the principality. 'Welcome to Wales.' As you explore Snowdonia by rail and on foot, you will experience this welcome at first hand. It is as invigorating as the mountain air.

SUMMIT OF SNOWDON.

# The railway history of Snowdonia

A long book would be needed to deal adequately with the history of Snowdonia's railways. This short chapter indicates the lines that survive, or have been closed and then reopened. More detailed accounts of each will be found later in this book.

The story begins in the reign of George IV. In 1824, the Assheton-Smiths, who owned the Dinorwic slate quarries above Llyn Padarn in the lovely Llanberis district, built a 2ft 0in gauge tramway. On this their slates were to be carried down by gravity to Port Dinorwic, on the Menai Straits, for shipment. *(See chapter 5).*

In the following year, the Nantlle Railway Company was incorporated. The company intended to build a similar tramway, though of 3ft 6in gauge, that would carry copper and slate from the Vale of Nantlle, on the west side of the mountain Elidir Fawr, to the quays at Caernarfon. Laying of the track was supervised by George and Robert Stephenson. The line was about nine miles long, and was ready for use by 1828. Horses were used to draw the wagons.

During the 1820s, Thomas Telford was employed to improve the London to Holyhead road, on which mail to and from Ireland depended. To overcome the worst hazards that faced the horse-drawn coaches — namely the River Conwy and the Menai Straits, both of which had to be crossed by ferry, with intolerable delays — Telford planned and built two great suspension bridges. Both were completed in 1826.

In 1836, the Ffestiniog Railway (1ft 11½ in gauge) was opened. It was to provide, in the words of the relevant Act of Parliament, "a more direct, easy, cheap and commodious communication between the interior of the principal slate and other quarries in the county of Merioneth and the various shipping places".

In those early days, the line relied mainly on horses which pulled the empty wagons from the harbour at Port Madoc up to Blaenau Ffestiniog. The horses then ran downhill in ease and comfort in their own containers as the trains, heavily laden with slates, sped smoothly down to the coast under the influence of gravity. The line is still in use today, and is one of Snowdonia's principal tourist attractions. *(See chapter 8).*

*Left: Early postcard showing Snowdon summit with the railway station and line just discernible on the right hand side*

While the advantages of steam-powered railways, over those that relied on horses or gravity, were becoming increasingly apparent, the Government in London was still trying to improve the mail service to Ireland. By 1840, the Cabinet was ready to support a scheme, put forward by George Stephenson, that would take a coastal railway line from Crewe to Holyhead. But, this project would need stronger bridges over the Conwy and the Menai Straits. Times were hard and money was short. Delays were inevitable. It was March 1850 before express passenger trains were able to travel on the whole of the Crewe to Holyhead line. *(See chapter 4.)*

Plans were being made, meanwhile, for other lines that would make travel and the transport of freight easier in and around Snowdonia.

In 1852 the Bangor and Caernarvon Company completed a single line (now closed). In 1853, a line that would join Llandudno to the Crewe to Holyhead line was authorised (it is still in use). In 1855, tenders were invited for the construction of a railway between Llanidloes and Newtown. The promoters saw the possibility of this becoming, eventually, part of a longer line that would join Manchester and Milford Haven.

The contract was awarded to David Davies of Llandinam, who subsequently became a railway builder of prime importance. Under Davies's direction, the Newtown to Oswestry line followed, and then the Newtown to Machynlleth and the Oswestry to Whitchurch, so that for the first time in their lives people from the Welsh Marches were within easy reach of the sea. In 1864 the lines amalgamated, being known for many years as The Cambrian Railways Company.

1858 saw the start of another great enterprise with the opening of the Knighton to Craven Arms Railway. This was to be the first part of the Central Wales Railway which, it was hoped, would run from Shrewsbury to Swansea. The second part of the line from Knighton to Llandrindod Wells was not in use until 1865.

In 1859, work started on the first part of the line that was to join Ruabon, Corwen, a junction station close to Bala, and Dolgellau. Four separate small companies undertook the construction of this line which ran, for part of its way, along the side of Bala Lake (Llyn Tegid). The later history of this beautiful line is told in chapter 13.

In 1860, the first section of the Conwy Valley branch line was laid down. It ran from Conwy to Llanrwst, and when the first train steamed up the valley press reporters were loud in their praise of the local scenery. Between 1865 and 1868 the line was extended to Betws-y-Coed, "a favourite haunt of the angler and artist" and, incidentally, of the tourist. Further extensions towards the slate-rich

Blaenau Ffestiniog followed, but slowly, as financial and geographical difficulties impeded progress. It was 1879 before the line could be called reasonably complete, and even then there was only an improvised station at the upper end. *(See chapter 7).*

In 1864, David Davies's former partner Thomas Savin was working hard on the grand Cambrian Coast line that he intended to build between Aberystwyth and Porth Dynllaen, to the north of Snowdonia. Two years later, Savin was bankrupt. The extraordinary development of this lovely line is described in chapter 10.

In 1865, another slate-carrying line — the Talyllyn Railway, with 2ft 3in gauge and a speed limit of 15 mph — opened for traffic along six miles of track between Tywyn and Abergynolwyn.

The later history of this line, much loved today by devotees of the charming Great Little Trains of Wales, is told in chapter 12.

Few of the lines opened in and around Snowdonia during the next two decades survived the closures of the 20th century. Gone are the Afon Wen to Caernarfon line (1867); the branch line from Caernarfon to Llanberis (1869); the Corris horse drawn tramway (provided with steam locomotives in 1879); the Bala to Blaenau Ffestiniog Railway (1882); and the North Wales Narrow Gauge Railway Company's 'General Undertaking' renamed, in 1922, The Welsh Highland Light Railway, though a short stretch of the last has been reopened. *(See chapter 9).*

Happily, two later lines are still in place for us to travel on — the Fairbourne and Barmouth Steam Railway, incorporated in 1890 *(chapter 11)* and the Snowdon Mountain Railway, opened in 1896; *(chapter 6).* The railway enthusiast can still find plenty to wonder at in this beautiful National Park.

*Train at Llanberis station on the Snowdon Mountain Railway, circa 1910*

*Coldstream Guardsman passes Penmaenmawr, 1962*

# The Crewe to Holyhead line

## 4

Many people travelling by rail to Snowdonia use British Rail's Crewe to Holyhead line from which you can alight at the popular coastal resorts of Prestatyn, Rhyl and Colwyn Bay which developed after the arrival of the railway. Closer to Snowdonia are the stations at Llandudno Junction, Conwy, Penmaenmawr, Llanfairfechan and Bangor. Overnight accommodation can normally be found in any of these towns except, possibly, at the height of the summer holiday season.

The line, mentioned briefly in chapter 3, came into existence in dramatic circumstances.

Construction started in 1845 — the first of the 'Railway Mania' years — when rival schemes for alternative routes to Holyhead were being vainly floated by several other companies.

By August 1846, more than 12,000 navigators (labourers) were hard at work. They had to contend with the wild sea waves of the North Wales coast; they had to make cuttings, embankments, viaducts and bridges; and they had to blast long tunnels through rock, slate and shale, which presented many new problems. Most of the men slept at night in roughly improvised huts close to the line they were bringing into being.

The greatest problems were encountered at Penmaenmawr. At this point, there was no room for a railway to be constructed between the massive, threatening headland and the sea. So, a terrace had to be carved out of rock face and an embankment raised in extremely perilous conditions. To protect them from boulders falling from above, covered ways had to be constructed at each end of the tunnel being blasted through the headland, making its total length more than a quarter of a mile. It took three years before the works on this part of the line were complete and ready for inspection.

The tunnel at Penmaenbach, between Conwy and Penmaenmawr, was, and is, no longer than the tunnel a little way to the west, but its excavation did not present quite so many dangers and difficulties. It was finished by November 1846: its opening was celebrated with elaborate ceremonies on land and on gaily decorated vessels off the shore.

In May 1847, there was a tragedy near Chester, when the Saltney end of Robert Stephenson's iron bridge over the Dee broke down under the weight of a train travelling over it. The carriages fell to the river bank below. Five passengers and the fireman were killed. This raised doubts among the general public about Robert Stephenson's competence. The directors of the company building the line continued to back him though, and work proceeded on the great bridges he was constructing for crossing the Conwy and the Menai Straits.

These bridges were designed in an entirely novel way — the trains were to run through long tubes made from iron plates held together by rivets. Robert Stephenson remembered that when he had first proposed a cast iron tubular bridge before a Parliamentary Committee "an incredulous glance of the most marked and unmistakable character was turned upon me by every honourable member". In spite of the Parliamentarians' doubts, Stephenson did not waver.

The Conwy bridge, needing to be shorter than the bridge over the Menai Straits and having to provide less clearance for tall masted sailing ships, was tackled first. The wrought iron tubes of which it was to be made were fabricated on the shores of the nearby estuary. When ready, they were moved into position between the bridge towers on floating pontoons then raised to the correct height by hydraulic presses.

The architect Francis Thompson designed the masonry of the bridge so that it would harmonise with Telford's suspension bridge and with the stonework of Edward I's castle behind.

Robert Stephenson's Britannia Bridge, built to carry the line over to Anglesey, was not so easy to complete: 19 lives were lost while the bridge was under construction. It was March 1850 before the first train, driven by Stephenson himself, was able to steam across the Straits. Queen Victoria soon arrived to admire the massive bridge with its striking combination of Egyptian and Grecian styles. On 23 May 1970, a fire rendered the bridge unusable and urgent plans were made for its repair. It is still regarded today as one of the major assets of North Wales.

# Suggested walks

## A walk through Conwy to Conwy mountain

The original Conwy station was designed to suit the stonework of the nearby railway bridge. It has been replaced by a modern "halt".

The town (which is sited just outside the boundaries of the Snowdonia National Park) is famed for its circuit of high defensive walls complete with three double-towered gates and 21 round towers. It was created for Edward 1 during 1283 to 1287, while his men were building the castle. In the process, the English king moved the Cistercian Abbey of Aberconwy, which had been occupying the site, to Maenan some eight miles upstream.

Edward's castle was splendidly placed on a rocky promontory and protected on three sides by the rivers Conwy and the smaller Gyffin, now little more than a stream. The complex can be roughly divided into two wards. The outer ward, nearest to the entrance from the town, is roughly rectangular. It contains the remaining fragments of the great hall, the kitchens, the bakehouse, the stockhouse used for punishments, and the prison tower with a gloomy dungeon. The smaller inner ward is dominated by the King's and Chapel Towers, which contained the well-protected royal apartments. There is a graceful oratory.

Conwy Castle played an important part in the struggles between the English and the Welsh. Here, in 1294, Edward was besieged and nearly forced to surrender. Richard 11 sought refuge here in 1399, but was taken away ignominiously to Flint, where he was, in effect, deposed by Henry Bolingbroke (later, Henry 1V). Both castle and town were captured in 1401 by the supporters of Owen Glendower. The castle changed hands twice during the Civil War, and was finally slighted, or reduced nearly to ruins, in 1665.

Three other buildings in Conwy are worth seeing. All are near the High Street.

St Mary's Church stands on the site once occupied by the Cistercian abbey. Parts of the fabric may once have belonged to the old abbey church. A tomb in the churchyard is said to have inspired Wordsworth's *We are Seven*, but there are doubts about the truth of this.

Plas Mawr was built as a prestigious town house by Robert Wynne of Gwydir, near Llanrwst, between 1577 and 1595. Most of the carved woodwork is original. The elaborate plaster ceilings are particularly notable. This charming little mansion is used now as the headquarters of the Royal Cambrian Academy of Art.

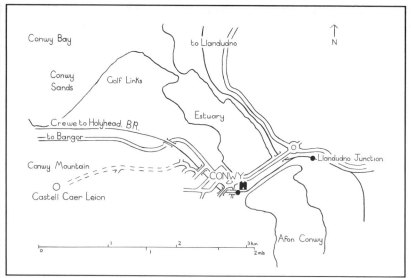

*Conwy's strategic position*

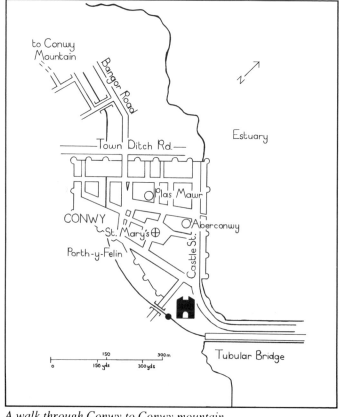

*A walk through Conwy to Conwy mountain*

Aberconwy, a house set cornerways-on to the High Street and Castle Street, was built of stone and timber at the beginning of the 16th century. It belongs to the National Trust. James Lees-Milne, visiting Aberconwy at the end of World War Two, described it as "deplorable". You may find it more to your taste.

To find your way to Conwy Mountain (Mynydd y Dref) with its fine views of the castle, town, sands and bay, with Anglesey in the distance, and (to the east) the Clwydian Hills, leave the town by following the Bangor Road through the fortified gate by the post office. Cross Mount Pleasant and the Town Ditch Road and walk straight ahead. 200 yards from the gate, turn left and walk over the bridge that crosses the railway. At the end of the bridge, take the road to the right. This leads to the clearly marked footpath by which the mountain can be safely approached.

There are ancient hut circles on Conwy Mountain, and traces of a hill fort (Caer Leion) can be seen at its summit. (808 ft). From here, you can retrace your steps to Conwy. (There is a path that leads in a southerly direction to the Sychnant Pass which used to accommodate horse-drawn vehicles travelling from Conwy to the little coastal town of Penmaenmawr. In summer, now, the road attracts too many motorists to make comfortable walking).

## A walk to Aber Falls

Sadly, no trains now stop at Aber. If you want to walk to Aber Falls, you can alight at Llanfairfechan BR station, which is about two miles east of Aber. Crosville buses run between the two towns.

Llanfairfechan is a quiet resort, with some simple and dignified buildings built in the early years of this century. The road from Llanfairfechan to Aber passes, on the left of the road, the picturesque house Pen-y-Bryn, built in the 17th century. Near this, close to the little River (or Afon) Aber, is Pen-y-Mwd, the Castle Mound. One of these is almost certainly the site of the vanished palace of the Princes of Gwynedd. According to tradition, it was here that Llywelyn the Great's wife Joan, daughter of King John, had a brief affair with one William de Braose. (William, for his gallantry, was promptly hanged). In 1282, it is known, Llywelyn the Last received here Edward I's demand that he should recognise the English king's sovereignty. Llywelyn's curt dismissal of this request led to the conquest of Wales.

The road from Aber to the Falls climbs through the Coedydd Aber Nature Reserve — a wooded glen with, on the east, the hill fort Maes-y-Gaer (730 ft) and, to the west, the hillside Ffridd Ddu (1,187 ft). The latter boasted a carefully tended rabbit warren until

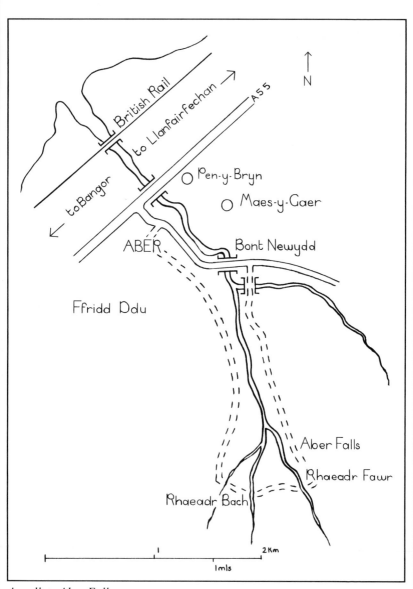

*A walk to Aber Falls*

the last years of the 19th century.

$^3/_4$ mile from Aber is Bont Newydd, where there are car parking facilities. From here, a nature trail can be followed for the next 1 $^1/_2$ miles. Clearly marked paths then lead uphill to Rhaeadr Fawr, where the water falls some 100ft more or less vertically, and to the smaller, less straightforward Rhaeadr Bach, $^1/_4$ mile or so to the west. Similar paths lead back to Aber. It is tempting to climb on towards the Carneddau, but the mountains ahead are for experienced walkers only.

## Journey to Llanberis

For the next stage of this exploration of Snowdonia, Llanberis makes an excellent centre. The town offers the popular Llanberis Lake Railway and the celebrated Snowdon Mountain Railway.

The nearest BR main line station to Llanberis is at Bangor (on the Crewe to Holyhead line). Bws Gwynedd bus services run from Bangor and from Caernarfon to Llanberis. If you are feeling energetic, you can use the country bus service operated by Deiniolen motors from Bangor bus station to Dinorwic. Alighting at the terminus at Dinorwic, you can descend on foot the famous 'Zig Zag' steps to Llanberis. The bus driver will point out the start of this route, much used as a short cut by local residents. From the steps, there are breathtaking views of the mountains on the other side of the valley, with the twin lakes Peris and Padarn lying below.

*Llanberis Lake Railway with the Snowdon range in the background*

# The Llanberis Lake Railway

## 5

## Rheilffordd Llyn Padarn

When the Assheton-Smiths built a seven mile long, 2ft 0in gauge tramway in 1824 to carry slates from their quarries near Llanberis to Port Dinorwic on the Menai Straits, they could not have foreseen that more than a century and half later the results of their creative thinking would still be giving incalculable pleasure to large numbers of visitors to North Wales.

Unfortunately for the enterprising quarry owners, their first tramway, which went through Deiniolen, had been badly engineered. It contained a number of awkward and undesirable inclines. So, in 1843, this was superseded by a 4ft 0in gauge line known as The Padarn Railway. The new line ran alongside the lake that gave it its name, and then by way of Pontrhythallt and Bethel to the slates' intended destination by the sea. The distance covered was 6 $5/_8$ miles.

In 1849, steam locomotives took the place of horses. Two 0-4-0 tender engines — the *Fire Queen*, built without a frame, and the *Jenny Lind* were acquired from Messrs Horlock of Northfleet, Kent. These remained in service until they, too, were superseded by the Hunslet 0-6-0 side tanks *Dinorwic* (1882) and *Pandora* (1886). A third Hunslet locomotive *Velinheli* was added in 1895. At the quarries and at the Port Dinorwic ends of the line, separate 1ft 10 $^3/_4$in gauge systems were operated by a number of busy little 0-4-0 locomotives. These were usually named after the most successful of the quarry owners' racehorses.

When Snowdonia's slate industry declined in the present century, as other roofing materials became more popular, the days of the Padarn line were clearly numbered. Workmen's trains continued to run daily on the line until 1947, and slate trains until 1961. Then the three Hunslet locomotives were disposed of, together with most of the rolling stock and the entire track. In 1969 the company went into liquidation.

The idea that part of the old railway might be re-opened under different private auspices was then mooted. The general plan, that a 1ft 11 $^1/_2$ in gauge track should be laid along the disused bed on the eastern side of the lake, was greeted locally with immense enthusiasm and much of the necessary funding came from people who lived and worked in the district.

Construction started in the autumn of 1970. First, the tangled thickets had to be cleared from the neglected route and new track put down. (Rails salvaged from the defunct quarries proved useful.) The line to be known as The Padarn Lake Railway or Rheilffordd Llyn Padarn, was opened in July 1971 when trains were able to travel as far as Cei Llydan. In that year, 60,672 passenger journeys were recorded.

In 1972, when the full run to Penllyn was in use, the number of passenger journeys had increased to 163,948.

All journeys now start and finish at Llanberis (Padarn) station, known locally as Gilfach Ddu. The approach road to the railway is clearly signposted off the main road at the south end of Llanberis. There is a useful shop at the station.

The trains are normally drawn by steam locomotives. The company is proud to own three 0-4-0 Hunslet saddle tanks: *Elidir*, built in 1889 and delivered new to the Dinorwic quarries (it was once called *Red Damsel*, in honour of a speedy horse); *Wild Aster*, built in 1904 and delivered new to the quarries; and *Dolbadarn* built in 1922 and first used for shunting at Port Dinorwic. The stock also includes *Helen Kathryn*, built in Germany in 1948; *Una*, which is really a museum piece; and there are a few supplementary diesel

*Elidir, a Hunslet saddle tank locomotive, on the Llanberis Lake Railway*

*Slate quarry near Llanberis*

locomotives.

Each train takes approximately 40 minutes for the return trip to Penllyn — four miles in all. Throughout its length it runs within the Padarn Country Park.

On the outward journey, the full magnificence of the main Snowdon range gradually unfolds. This section of the line runs on a ledge built right on the shore of the lake. Round the sharp Ladas curve, Nant Wen (The White Valley) opens up on the right with the village of Dinorwic visible high above the line. At Volcano Cutting, the trains pass through rocks which are actually solidified lava. Beyond these are less dramatic formations in which, in recent years, cables from the massive hydro-electric generating station hidden in the mountain Elidir Fawr have been carefully concealed.

The return journey from Penllyn is interrupted by a short stop at Cei Llydan station, the halfway point. It is possible to leave the train here, and let it return to Llanberis. You can catch the next train that calls at Cei Llydan, and, in the meantime, there will be plenty to see. A picture board helps visitors to identify every visible summit around. There are picnic sites by the lake.

# Suggested walks

Close to the Lake Railway station is the Welsh Slate Museum, housed in the former quarry workshops. This is well worth a visit, as it contains some impressive examples of early industrial equipment, including slate-cutting machinery and the largest water wheel ever used in Wales.

Many acres of land nearby, once devoted almost entirely to quarry work, have been designated The Padarn Country Park. Much of this is oak woodland, of an ancient type, that overlooks the lake. It can be explored by the numerous footpaths created over the years by quarrymen walking to and from their work. These paths have been clearly waymarked by Gwynedd County Council, and useful leaflets describing recommended routes can be obtained from the Information Centre close to the Lake Railway station.

The most notable walks are:

## The Vivian Trail walk

This starts at the large country park sign near the Lake Railway station. It leads to the Vivian Quarry, named after W W Vivian, the

*The Welsh Slate Centre at Gilfach Ddu, Llanberis*

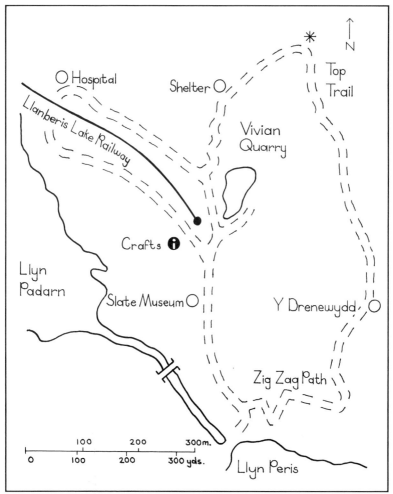

*Walks from Gilfach Ddu, Llanberis*

slate company's manager in the late 19th century. The quarry was closed in 1964 and the manager's office is now used as a craft workshop. Since then, the pit or sinc at the bottom of the quarry has filled with water to a depth of 50 feet. From the edge of the quarry, the trail leads to one of the slate-dressing areas, with the walia, or buildings, in which some of the men worked. Beyond is the quarry hospital in which injured men were treated. The old hospital mortuary can still be seen in a corner of the hospital garden. The hospital is used now as a visitors' centre. The last few 100 yards of this trail brings walkers close to the track of the Lake Railway. The trail ends with fine views of the Vivian Quarry Pool.

# The Vivian Top Trail

This is slightly longer than the last route recommended. (An hour and a half would be a reasonable time to allow). It takes walkers up the ascending levels at the side of the quarry, and past a 'dry' (uncemented) slate shelter in which the workers used to take refuge while blasting was being carried out. The path, later, comes down past the ruins of the quarrymen's temporary dwellings, (the Anglesey Barracks or Y Drenewydd, the new town). Then, by means of the zig zag path mentioned earlier, it brings the walker back to Gilfach Ddu.

A self-guided walk right round Llyn Padarn is described in a leaflet obtainable from the Information Centre. The walk is five miles long, takes approximately three hours, and, in places, is very difficult to follow. There is also a carefully organised nature trail.

Only a short walk from the Information Centre is the largest pumped storage power station in Europe. Tours of Dinorwig, as this power station is called, start from the Museum of the North, where the exhibition *Power of Wales* is to be found. Here, the history of Wales down the centuries is graphically explained.

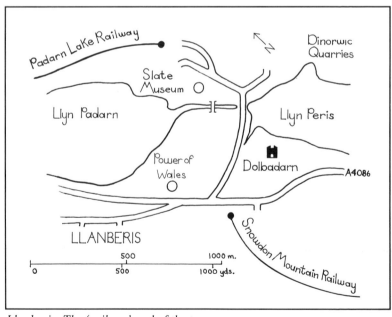

*Llanberis: The 'railway' end of the town*

# The Snowdon Mountain Railway

## 6

The Snowdon Mountain Railway can be boarded at about $^3/_4$ mile from the starting point of the Llanberis Lake Railway at Gilfach Ddu. The small station is at the south end of the town of Llanberis, close to the A4086 Caernarfon to Capel Curig road.

The train journey from Llanberis to the summit of Snowdon — $4 \, ^5/_8$ miles — takes approximately an hour. Each train waits empty at the summit for $^1/_2$ hour before leaving again for the descent to Llanberis. The downhill journey also lasts about an hour. So you have to allow a total of $2 \, ^1/_2$ hours for the return trip.

A word of warning is necessary here. Snowdon has the most variable and, probably, treacherous weather conditions of any high ground in the British Isles. The summit is less than ten miles from the Irish Sea, and gale force winds can blow up in a matter of minutes. Inevitably, temperatures at the summit are liable to be

*Directors and staff of the engineering company which constructed the Snowdon Mountain Railway. Ladas was named after Laura Alice Duff Assheton-Smith, wife of the local estate owner. (SMR)*

considerably lower than those prevailing at Llanberis. Suitable clothing and footwear **must** be worn if considerable hardship and danger are to be avoided.

The Snowdon Mountain Railway is Britain's only rack and pinion line. (The name comes from the pinions on the driving axles of the locomotives that engage with the teeth of a rack positioned between the rails).

This method of ensuring the security necessary for travelling up and down steep gradients was first developed at the Middleton Colliery in Yorkshire in 1812. It was used later, during the 1860's, by a railway that took passengers to the summit of the 6,293 ft Mount Washington in the United States. Then, in 1871, a rack and pinion railway up Mount Rigi in Switzerland was constructed by Niklaus Riggenbach — and improved to the designs of Dr Roman Abt.

The possibility of a comparable railway to the summit of Snowdon was then discussed, but it was not until the Snowdon Mountain

Tramroad and Hotels Company was formed in November 1894 that the dream started to turn into reality.

Construction of the line proceeded rapidly after that, and the line was declared open, amid great rejoicing, on Easter Monday 1896. The festivities were marred, however, when the locomotive *Ladas* left the track when returning from the summit and ran over the edge of a precipice. The coaches, which were equipped with brakes, were brought to a halt but two passengers in a panic jumped from the train and one of them, the landlord of the Padarn Villa Hotel at Llanberis, died of his injuries. The railway was closed at once, so that the rack system could be modified. The line was reopened for passenger traffic in the following year and was immediately successful. More than 12,000 passengers were taken up Snowdon in the first full season.

Today, each passenger train is made up of a locomotive and one coach with a capacity of 59 passengers. The locomotive moves chimney first up the mountain, pushing the coach in front of it. For reasons of safety, the coach is not coupled to the locomotive. There are, today, ten locomotives on the line: four steam-powered engines built in Switzerland in 1895-6; three built in 1922-3; and three diesel locomotives added since 1986.

A sharp ascent begins soon after the station is left. A viaduct is crossed from which a fine view of the Ceunant Mawr Falls can be enjoyed. There is a passing place at Hebron (930 ft). After that the line climbs the long northerly spur of Snowdon, giving excellent views of Moel Eilio and Y Foel Goch. There is a second passing place at Halfway (1,600 ft). To the right is the deep Cwm Brwynog (Valley of Rushes) with its spectacular cliffs. The third passing place is at Clogwyn (2,550 ft). Beyond Clogwyn, you can glimpse, to the left, a brief view of the rocky cleft known as Cwm Glas Bach, with, beyond it, the Pass of Llanberis. The line then bears to the right, passing above the cliffs of Clogwyn Coch (The Red Cliff). Clogwyn du'r Arddu is over to the right. Climbs on these cliffs are described in the most authoritative guide books as "very difficult". It is easy to understand why.

The summit of Snowdon, with its cafe, mailing facilities and tourists, is sometimes disparaged by those who prefer less accessible and therefore lonelier places, but no one can dispute the magnificence of the views that can be obtained from here on a clear day. The complete mountain and hill system of North Wales, with no fewer than 20 lakes, can be studied, as can Anglesey, lying like a flat cut-out shape in the wide expanses of the Irish Sea. The mountains of the Lake District, nearly 100 miles away, are visible to the north-north-east; the Isle of Man, 85 miles away, to the north-

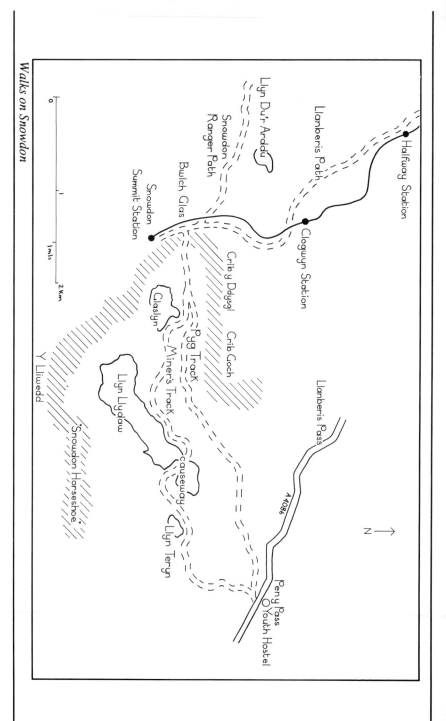

Walks on Snowdon

west; and the Wicklow Mountains, in Ireland, between 80 and 90 miles away in a westerly direction.

The unpredictable nature of the weather conditions on Snowdon has been mentioned already. If winds are too strong, or if there is a risk of the track being affected by snow or ice, train services have to terminate at Clogwyn Station (approximately $^3/_4$ of the way to the summit), or even occasionally at Rocky Valley Halt. The round trip to Clogwyn and back lasts just under two hours which includes a half-hour halt at Clogwyn.

# Suggested walks

It is difficult to make firm recommendations about walks on Snowdon without taking into consideration the weather, the age and physical condition of the walkers, and their general awareness of how to behave in high altitude conditions. It should be clearly stated though, that each year there are far too many nasty accidents on the mountain caused mainly by walkers being too casual about their equipment or the weather. It is important to set off as early as possible in the morning to avoid getting into difficulties as darkness falls. Walkers should always leave word at their hotel, bed and breakfast house, or camp site of where they intend to go and roughly at what time they expect to return. A good map is essential.

## Return walk by the Llanberis track to Llanberis

This walk, which follows the well-marked track originally used in the 19th century by visitors on hired ponies, provides by far the easiest of the descents. The path is never far from the mountain railway line, though occasional divergences will be noted — as at Bwlch Glas, approximately $^1/_4$ mile from the Summit station — to exceptionally well-sited viewpoints. A shortened form of this walk, starting at Clogwyn, should be fairly easily managed by the average family.

There are at least four other unmarked routes by which descents from the summit of Snowdon can be made on foot, but they should be attempted only by fit and experienced walkers. Possible difficulties with transport should be taken into consideration, too; none of these routes leads to a railway station, and buses in the more remote parts of Snowdonia are not plentiful. It is most useful to know about the Snowdon Sherpa bus service which runs from early summer to the autumn with a reduced service in winter. These buses go from Llanberis to Penygwryd and back, stopping at the Pen y Pass Youth Hostel, and there are extensions and connecting services to Capel Curig, Betws-y-Coed, Beddgelert, and other centres. The Sherpa bus service is very useful to anyone wishing to climb Snowdon by one route and descend via another and, of course, the service is designed to help you visit Snowdonia without the use of a car.

Up-to-date information about the Sherpa services and other bus services linking with them can be obtained from Tourist Information offices in North Wales, or by post with a 9in x 6in stamped addressed envelope from the National Parks Office, Penrhyndeudraeth, Gwynedd, LL48 6LS.

If, then, you have checked on the available buses and are feeling confident enough to explore these majestic slopes, these are the routes in, approximately, the reverse order of difficulty. All share a common path, close to the railway, from the summit as far down as Bwlch Glas.

## The Snowdon Ranger track

This path diverges to the north-west at Bwlch Glas. It leads down the steep ridge of Clogwyn Du'r Arddu to Bwlch Cwm Brwynog (1600 ft). From there, the track passes between Moel Cynghorion, on the right, and, on the left, the boggy expanses of Cwm Clogwyn which contain a reservoir and four small lakes. The track leads down ultimately to the Snowdon Ranger hostel, which is by Llyn Cwellyn, and the A4085 Caernarfon to to Beddgelert road. (At least 2 $^1/_2$ hours should be allowed for this walk.)

## The Pyg track

This path diverges to the north-east at Bwlch Glas. Look out for the standing marker stone. The Pyg track was given its name, according to one theory, by Victorian climbers staying at the Pen-y-Gwryd Hotel at the head of the nearby Nant-y-Gwryd Valley. The track leads the walker into the cwm that contains the beautiful lake Glaslyn, in a fine glacial cirque, and then down the hillside below the steep crags of Crib Goch (The Red Comb). From the track, Llyn Llydaw and the sheer cliffs of Yr Wyddfa and Lliwedd provide a succession of impressive views. Close to the north-eastern end of Llyn Llydaw, the track passes Bwlch Moch (1,850 ft). This can be translated Pig's Pass, and has been thought by some pundits to provide an alternative explanation for the name of the track.

This descent ends at the Pen-y-Pass Youth Hostel, which is at the head of the Llanberis Pass, and on the A4086 road. (Allow 2 $^1/_2$ hours.)

## The Miners' track

This path also diverges to the north east at Bwlch Glas. The Pyg track and the Miners' track coincide then for about 700 yards, when the latter diverges to the right and leads down to the north bank of the lake Glaslyn. Near Glaslyn, it passes the disused copper workings that once gave employment to the men commemorated by the track's name. The track then skirts the north shore of Llyn Llydaw (1,416 ft) for about $^1/_2$ mile, crosses the end of the lake by means of a causeway, and heads downhill to the north side of the smaller Llyn Teryn (1,238 ft). From here, the track leads down to the Youth Hostel at Pen-y-Pass.

*Farm near Pen-y-Gwryd*

# 7 | The Conwy Valley line

After reaching the summit of its highest mountain, you may think that any further exploration of Snowdonia will be an anticlimax. This is far from being the case.

To sample some of Snowdonia's other major attractions, you have only to make your way back from Llanberis to Llandudno Junction station. To do this, you can return by bus to Bangor. Then, along part of BR's Holyhead to Crewe line to 'The Junction', as Llandudno Junction station is often called locally.

The Conwy Valley branch line, which starts at Llandudno Junction, was only intended, at first, to take travellers as far as the thriving market town Llanrwst. The extended line was a long time — 19 years — in the making. (An abbreviated account of its construction is included in chapter 3. )

The initial delays concerned the first ten miles of track, from

*A diesel railcar enters Llanrwst and Trefriw, 1966.  (C L Caddy/Colour Rail)*

Llandudno Junction to Trefriw. On which side of the river, wide and tidal here, should the railway run? After much controversy, the east bank was chosen. This part of the line, with stations at Glan Conwy (then called Llansaintffraid), Tal-y-Cafn (later, Tal-y-Cafn and Eglwysbach), and the intended terminus at Llanrwst (later, Llanrwst and Trefriw) was opened for passenger traffic in 1863. The river at Tal-y-Cafn had to be crossed, at the time, by a ferry. Understandably, numbers of sightseeing tourists wished to cross over into Caernarfonshire (now, Gwynedd). Public demand soon made the construction of a road bridge here essential.

Victorian travellers to the Conwy Valley were urged to visit Trefriw, and to take the spa water there for the sake of their health. Betws-y-Coed, a few miles upstream, was increasing in popularity too, as a centre for tourism, and by 1868 the Conwy Valley railway line had been extended as far as that previously rather isolated little town. Betws expanded rapidly after the arrival of the railway and became — as it still is — a favourite holiday resort. From the town, the beautiful valleys of the Upper Conwy, the Lledr and the Llugwy can be exhaustively explored.

The possible extension of the line above Betws-y-Coed and up the lovely Lledr Valley to Blaenau Ffestiniog was considered next. This offered the railway company a tempting chance to cash in on the slate-carrying trade, but the construction of the line presented almost insuperable difficulties. Plans for the line were not finally approved until 1872. The railway directors had not been dragging their feet — they had simply been afraid of committing themselves to a hugely expensive and possibly unprofitable undertaking. Climbing steeply up the southern slopes of the Lledr Valley, with as many curves as a slippery snake, the line had to be taken somehow through the daunting mass of Moel Dyrnogydd (2,510 ft).

Extreme measures were called for. The northern end of the line was to be extended as quickly as possible to the side of the mountain to facilitate the carriage of the materials needed by the tunnellers. A local inn had its licence taken away, lest its premises should prove distracting to the men involved in the construction of the line. A hospital fund was set up, and a surgeon retained. The Vicar of Dolwyddelan was given bibles and prayer books and was paid by the railway company for ministering to the tunnellers' spiritual needs. At last, in 1878, after explosions, rock falls, floodings, and other mishaps — some of them fatal — the great tunnel was complete. It measures approximately 3,800 yards long and at its highest point is 790 feet above sea level.

It would be hard to find a more charming section of any branch line than the one that still carries passenger trains, in spite of all threats of closure, beside the tumultuous Lledr, between the Junction Pool above Betws-y-Coed and the Moel Dyrnogydd tunnel. There are alighting points in this idyllic landscape at Pont-y-Pant, where the Romans who made the road Sarn Helen used to cross the river, at Dolwyddelan, and at Roman Bridge. Between the further end of the Moel Dyrnogydd tunnel and Blaenau Ffestiniog there are landscapes of a very different kind.

At Blaenau Ffestiniog, the BR Conwy Valley line connects with the Ffestiniog Narrow Gauge Railway, which is the subject of the next chapter.

# Suggested walks

## Walk to Bodnant Gardens

Alight at Tal-y-Cafn. Turn left outside the station for a short walk up the busy A470 road to the entrance of these world-famous gardens.

The gardens, with their panoramic views of Snowdonia, were laid out in the last decades of the 19th century by Henry Pochin, an industrialist of means, who had a passionate interest in trees and horticulture. His great work was carried on by his daughter and her husband, the first Lord Aberconway. More extensions to the gar-

*View of the Conwy Valley from above Roewen*

dens were made by the second Lord Aberconway who gave the greater part of them to the National Trust in 1949, and by his son the third Lord. The gardens contain a celebrated series of terraces, collections of rare rhododendrons, azaleas, and other covetable specimens, and an elegant 18th century Pin Mill, brought here from Gloucestershire shortly before World War Two to act as a garden house.

## Walk to the Pass of Bwlch-y-Ddeufaen

Tal-y-Cafn station is the starting point of this walk also. The distance to be covered — 4 $^1/_2$ miles to the top of the pass, and as many back — will need a measure of stamina, but the route recommended is pleasant for all of its length. 'Turn back when you think best' is the name of the game.

Begin by crossing the river by the bridge mentioned earlier. (If sheep are being sold by auction in the sale yard close to the bridge's approach road, a few minutes can be instructively spent in watching some of the local farmers at their business.)

Then follow the road up the hill to the village of Tyn-y-Groes. Cross over the B5106, and follow the undulating minor road ahead through fields and woods until a steep slope leads down to level ground and, more or less, straight ahead to Roewen (sometimes spelled Ro Wen). This has won awards for being one of the best kept villages in Gwynedd. Walk through the village. Where the road forks at the far end, take the road to the right.

There is then a long climb up the lower slopes of Tal-y-Fan (2,000 ft). Beyond the small farms Buarth and Isallt, there are astonishing views of the high moorlands of the county of Clwyd. A little way past the isolated Youth Hostel at Rhiw, the road — now no more than a track — passes, on the bare mountainside, the stone slabs that are all that is left of an ancient burial chamber. To the left and south, the sky line leads up to the Iron Age hill fort now known as Pen-y-Gaer. From here, the native inhabitants of the valley would have looked down on the Roman encampment, Canovium, set up on level ground close to the River Conwy. The place is known now as Caerhun.

It is certain that the Romans used the pass of Bwlch-y-Ddeufaen as a convenient way of reaching the coast. The eighth Roman milestone from Canovium is now in the British Museum.

The pass was given its name to celebrate two big standing stones near the top. The rocks scattered close to these are said, in tales told to the local children, to have fallen from the skirt of a giantess. She was striding towards Anglesey and intended to use

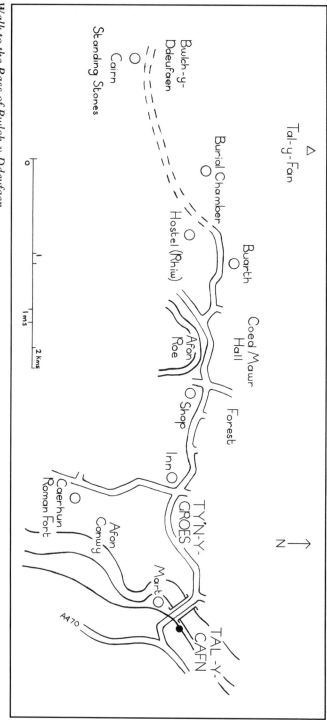

Walk to the Pass of Bwlch-y-Ddeufaen

the boulders as stepping stones with which to cross the Menai Straits. According to the legend, she became too tired to carry them further, so had to let them drop.

From the standing stones, a path leads down to Llanfairfechan. (This makes an alternative to the return walk to Tal-y-Cafn).

## A walk to Trefriw

For this, alight at Llanrwst station. From the station, a footpath leads to the Gower bridge over the Conwy. *(See sketch map)*. From the bridge, the path leads in a straight line to the little town of Trefriw, which has a remarkable church said to have been built by Llywelyn the Great to save himself the uphill journey to another, and older, church about a mile away.

At Trefriw, you can visit the popular Woollen Mills, where bed-spreads, tweeds and other goods are manufactured from raw wool. All traditional processes — blending, willowing, carding, spinning, dyeing, warping and weaving — are carried out on the premises, and there is a well-stocked shop.

About 1 $^1/_4$ miles north of Trefriw, and to be approached by walking (if you care to) along the B5106 Trefriw to Dolgarrog road, you will find the Victorian pump room and bath house of Trefriw Spa. Here, the Romans are known to have exploited the waters which are exceptionally rich in iron oxide (for bathing) and sulphur (for drinking). The spa, closed for some years, has recently been re-opened and visitors are able to enter the ancient Grotto of Wells where the strongly-flavoured healing waters rise.

## Walk to the Gwydir Forest

For this, you should also alight at Llanrwst station. On this occasion, walk through the delightful little town.

Llanrwst was for centuries one of the most important market towns of North Wales. It has been famous for harp makers, too. One of them, David Cae Ceiliog, lived in the early 19th century in the old almshouses by the river. It is said that he would never finish a harp in the almshouses in case the chattering of the old women there should spoil the sweet tone of the instrument. Instead, he preferred to work on a flat stone by the side of the Conwy.

On the far side of the town from the BR station is the Parish Church of St Grwst. This contains a fine rood screen and loft brought from Maenan Abbey when Henry VIII dissolved the coun-try's monasteries. The adjoining chapel was built as a burial place for members of the Wynne family of Gwydir. In it is a large stone coffin that may once have contained the body of Llywelyn the Great.

Cross the river by the graceful 'Quaking Bridge'. It is believed this was designed in the early 17th century by Inigo Jones. Reinforced to take the strains of modern traffic, the bridge has lost its former tendency to vibrate.

Close to the bridge, on the west bank of the river, there is a small 15th century stone building known as Tu Hwnt i'r Bont. This was once used as the district's court house. It is now owned by the National Trust.

Walking westwards, away from the river, you will see ahead romantic Gwydir Castle, sheltered by great cedar trees planted to commemorate the wedding of Charles I. It was built in the 16th and 17th centuries around an earlier hall, and was enlarged in the 19th century. At one time it was the home of the tyrannical Sir John Wynne (1553-1627). The castle was gutted by fire twice — in 1912 and 1922 — but it was painstakingly restored later by the late Arthur Clegg and his son. Gwydir Castle is particularly noted for its resident peacocks. A stroll in the grounds is an unforgettable experience.

To the west of Gwydir Castle, on the other side of the Trefriw to Betws-y-Coed road, there is the extensive Gwydir Forest, managed

*The so-called 'quaking bridge' at Llanrwst*

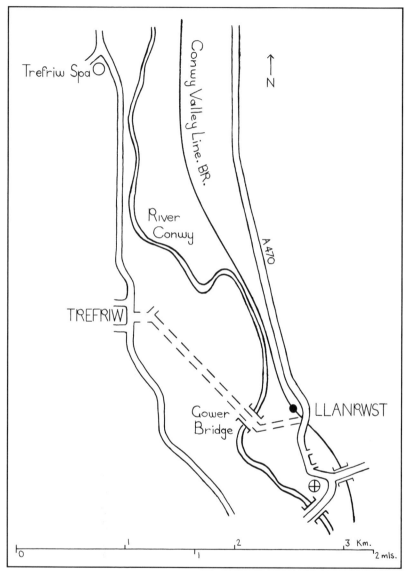

*A walk to Trefriw*

by the Forestry Commission. Close to the road are Gwydir Uchaf House and Gwydir Uchaf Chapel, the former now used as Forestry Commission offices, and to house an exhibition.

Information can be obtained here, as at the National Park Visitor Centre, Betws-y-Coed, about walks in the forest. The most popular

*Stocks in the grounds of Gwydir Castle*

are the clearly marked round trail known as Lady Mary's Walk (one mile) and the longer Drws Gwyn (White Door) trail. The latter leads along paths and forest roads to Llyn Parc, a lake once artificially deepened and used to supply water to the defunct Aberllyn mine. From the lake, the trail leads down through the charming Aberllyn Ravine to the car park at Pont-y-Pair, close to Betws-y-Coed. A cave above the track sheltered the local outlaw Dafydd ap Siencyn when he was on the run during the Wars of the Roses. The bridge over the River Llugwy at Pont-y-Pair may have been constructed as far back as the 15th century.

*Pont-y-Pair near Betws-y-Coed*

*Gateway at Gwydir Castle*

# Walks around Betws-y-Coed

Close to the BR station at Betws-y-Coed there is a most interesting Railway Museum. Worth seeing too is the Waterloo Bridge at the other end of the town, which carries the A5 road over the Conwy. Designed by Thomas Telford, and made by William Hazeldine, this elegant iron arch owes its name to the fact that it was put up in 1815, the year of the famous battle.

It is possible to explore the surrounding countryside on foot by obtaining the leaflets *12 Walks in the Gwydir Forest* available at the National Park Visitor Centre. Several of these will lead you up and out of the forest into open moorlands and lakes.

*A walk in the Gwydir Forest*

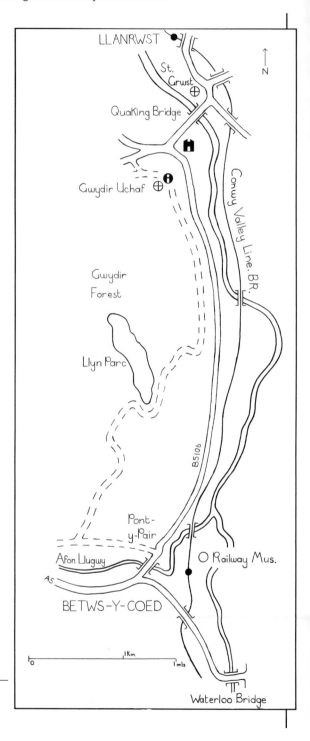

LLANRWST

St. Grwst

Quaking Bridge

Gwydir Uchaf

Conwy Valley Line. BR.

Gwydir Forest

Llyn Parc

B5106

Pont-y-Pair

O Railway Mus.

Afon Llugwy

A5

BETWS-Y-COED

1Km

0

1mls

Waterloo Bridge

N

# Walks to Dolwyddelan Castle

Dolwyddelan makes a splendid centre for an exploration, on foot, of the delightful Lledr Valley.

For a comparatively short walk to Dolwyddelan Castle, alight at Dolwyddelan BR Halt. The road to the village of Dolwyddelan crosses the Lledr by means of a small bridge. Then it passes the very small and primitive 'old' church. This was built in the 16th century to replace a less easily defended earlier church.on another site. It has a chapel on the south side which was added by Robert Wynne. His town house, Plas Mawr, was noticed in Conwy.

*Dolwyddelan Castle*

When you reach the main Betws-y-Coed to Blaenau Ffestiniog road, turn left. Dolwyddelan Castle is sited just over a mile from the village. It stands dramatically on a rocky bluff just to the right of the road. The keep was built in the 12th century, probably by Iorwerth, father of Llywelyn the Great. (Llywelyn may have been born here, and he certainly used the place in later life as one of his residences). With its crumbled west tower and curtain walls, this is one of the most romantic ruins in Snowdonia.

Dolwyddelan and the fields and enclosures around are dominated by the noble profile of Moel Siabod (2,861 ft). There are footpaths that can be followed, with some difficulty, for a little of the way up the bleak expanses to the north of the village. However, this part of the range is best avoided by walkers.

At Blaenau Ffestiniog, beyond the famous Moel Dyrnogydd tunnel, you can change from BR's Conwy Valley line to the narrow gauge Ffestiniog Railway *(see chapter 8)*. But, before you leave Blaenau Ffestiniog, you may care to visit the award-winning Llechwedd Slate Caverns. A bus service runs to Llechwedd from

Blaenau Ffestiniog BR station.

In the caverns visitors can ride on the Miners' tramway along the original route used by the miners in 1846. On the Deep Mine Tour, visitors ride on the steepest incline encountered on any passenger-carrying railway in Britain.

Close to Blaenau Ffestiniog is the Gloddfa Ganol Slate Mine. Here, visitors can explore more than half a mile of tunnels and chambers of the old mine workings. There are also a mining museum, a natural history museum, and a mine transport museum in which a number of historic narrow gauge locomotives are displayed.

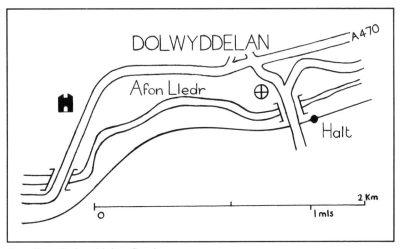

*A walk to Dolwyddelan Castle*

*Norman Gurley*

*Merddin Emrys steams its way along the Ffestiniog Railway*

One of the most impressive civil engineering feats of the early 19th century was the construction of a mile-long cob across the estuary of the Glaslyn, on the west coast of North Wales. This was planned and carried out by William Madocks, MP for Boston in Lincolnshire, who had bought land in the district.

Madocks's enterprise involved the reclamation of more than 7,000 acres of land from the sea. He also developed a harbour by the cob around which grew the little town known as Port Madoc (now Porthmadog).

The possibility of bringing slates down from the mountains to Port Madoc on a railway of some kind was discussed for some years. Madocks himself put forward a scheme. Action was at last taken by Samuel Holland, the owner of slate quarries at Rhiw, inland from Port Madoc. One day, Holland met Henry Archer, an Irish barrister who had retired from legal work, in an inn. Archer did not enjoy being idle, and he told Holland so. Holland then suggested that he and Archer should consider the possibility of bringing his slates down to the sea in wagons instead of on the backs of pack animals. The two men first explored the wild terrain together on New Year's Day, 1830.

Their next step was to approach the engineer James Spooner, who had worked with William Madocks on the construction of his great cob. Guided by Spooner, they applied to Parliament for powers to make a railway or tramroad from Port Madoc to the slate quarries near Ffestiniog. An Act of 1832 gave them those powers. Most of the money needed for the construction of the line was provided by Archer's Irish friends.

Spooner's railway, nearly 14 miles long, had a gauge of 1ft $11^{1}/_{2}$ in. It was engineered most successfully. By providing wide loops and carefully placed slate embankments, the overseer managed to avoid steep gradients in the 700ft descent. The most noticeable gradient was 1 in 79, which posed no real problems. The opening of the railway brought increased prosperity to Port Madoc, and in the mountains slate production soared.

By the time Charles Easton Spooner, James's son, took charge of the railway in 1856, the horse and gravity system of propulsion was plainly out of date. The use of steam locomotives on a line of so narrow a gauge had been thought impracticable though, and, by law, passengers could not be carried on new railways of less than the British Standard gauge. Charles Spooner was not discouraged. In 1863 he ordered four small steam locomotives from George England and Co. of Hatcham. At the same time, he obtained permission from the Board of Trade to run passenger trains on the line — the first to be allowed on a narrow gauge railway anywhere in the

*The railway crosses the turbulent Afon Cwmorthin*

world.

The locomotives Spooner had commissioned, *Princess* and *Prince*, delivered in 1863, and *Mountaineer* and *Palmerston*, brought into service in the following year, were very successful. Each could draw a train with 200 passengers up the line at a speed of 10-12 m.p.h. In 1867, two slightly larger locomotives *Welsh Pony* and *Little Giant* were added. But, by that time, the limitations of a single line enterprise were apparent. Faced with the need to double the track, which would be costly, Spooner turned to the engineer Robert Fairlie. He asked Fairlie to devise a locomotive that could pull longer trains and so improve the capacity of the line.

Fairlie had a problem. How could he design a more powerful locomotive that would move heavier loads on the Ffestiniog line and, at the same time, travel without derailments round its sinuous curves? He found a brilliantly original solution: the double-bogie articulated *Little Wonder*. This looked like two locomotives mounted back to back, with a chimney at each end and a cab in the middle.

The revolutionary design caused a sensation, and brought railroad executives to the Ffestiniog line from around the world. In 1871 a gold medallion and silver shield were awarded to Spooner by the Emperor of Russia.

Before long, the company was producing, in fully equipped workshops at Boston Lodge — near the end of Madocks's cob — its own Fairlie engines. The line was soon to face competition though.

Standard gauge lines constructed principally to carry slates from Blaenau Ffestiniog to Llandudno Junction and from Blaenau to Bala started to take much of the Ffestiniog line's freight traffic. Passengers, except in holiday seasons, were scarce. The difficulties of the slate industry in the early decades of this century accelerated the company's decline; the increasing popularity of the motor car hastened its decease. The railway closed in 1946 after years of terminal decrepitude. The buildings, track and rolling stock were then grievously vandalised.

The basic qualities of the old railway were not forgotten though. The railway enthusiast Allan Garraway, who worked for BR's Eastern Region, explored part of the track with a friend, and they decided that the Ffestiniog Railway was just as worthy of restoration as the Talyllyn line, on which much work had already been done by enthusiastic volunteers.

So, in 1951, a rescue committee was formed. The debt-ridden company that still officially owned the railway was approached, but there was not enough money available to buy out the company's interests. Then, in 1954, Alan Pegler, a member of the board of BR's Eastern Region, offered to buy the controlling shares, and to let the railway be revived by a society of volunteers. This society was later replaced by the Ffestiniog Railway Trust, a registered charity that acts as a majority shareholder.

Between June 1955, when Alan Garraway gave up his job with British Rail and became manager of the Ffestiniog Railway, and 1957, when the line was in operation as far as Penrhyn, teams of unpaid workers helped restore the track. Trees had to be felled and thickets cleared and long-lost wagons found and re-built. The number of passengers carried rose as the line lengthened and as interest in it increased. Most of the trains at that time were powered by *Prince*, one of the line's original locomotives.

It was hoped that by the early 1970s the line would be usable as far as Tanygrisiau, 12 miles from Porthmadog and only a few 100 yards from the original terminus at Blaenau Ffestiniog. There was, however, a snag. While the line had been out of use, the British Electricity Authority had built, near Tanygrisiau, a pumped storage installation designed to boost the grid at times of peak demand. The authority did not want a railway line used by tourists to run close to their installation, and they took legal action to prevent this. After much aggravation, an alternative route for the railway, to the west of the Tanygrisiau reservoir, was agreed. The line was to have, at Ddaullt, a great spiral (The Deviation). By this, the railway would cross over itself, gaining the 35ft extra height needed for the line to pass behind the power station two miles further on.

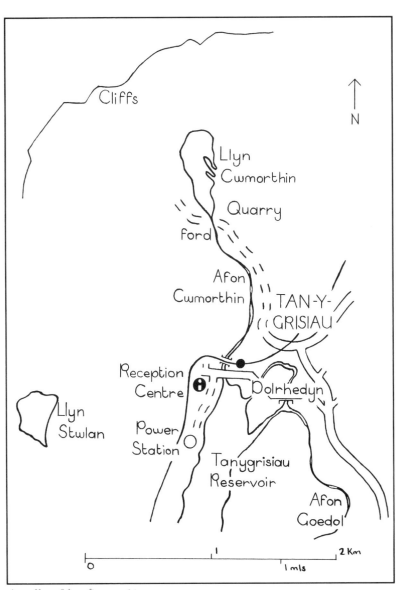

*A walk to Llyn Cwmorthin*

By 1982, the deviation was complete; a new tunnel, 287 yards long, had been made at Moelgwyn; bridges had been built to carry the line over the power station water pipes; and the Ffestiniog Railway was able to run once again all the way from Porthmadog to Blaenau Ffestiniog. The station at Blaenau Ffestiniog was officially opened by the Rt.Hon. George Thomas MP (then Speaker of the House of Commons and, later, Viscount Tonypandy) on 30 April 1983. The line is now one of the most successful tourist attractions in North Wales.

# Suggested walks

There are five regular stopping places on the Ffestiniog Railway between Blaenau Ffestiniog and the terminus at Porthmadog. They are Tanygrisiau, Dduallt, Tan-y-Bwlch, Penrhyn and Minffordd. (Here, they are listed in the order in which they will be encountered on a journey from Blaenau Ffestiniog to the sea. If you are travelling from the terminus at Porthmadog to Blaenau Ffestiniog, the order will, of course, be reversed.)

From each of these stopping places, there are enjoyable walks.

The company has produced a useful leaflet: *Where to go and What to do from Ffestiniog Railway Stations*. With a Ffestiniog Railway ticket you can break your journey wherever and whenever you wish.

## Walks from Tanygrisiau

The celebrated pumped hydro-electric power station, opened on 10 August 1963 by HM The Queen, is well worth a visit. The reception centre for visitors is close to the Ffestiniog Railway station. At the power station, beside the Tanygrisiau reservoir, visitors can see how water flows down from the upper reservoir, Llyn Stwlan, and drives the generators, which reach full power in less than a minute. The water is pumped back in off-peak periods.

For an enjoyable longer walk, turn right after the reception centre on to the Stwlan Dam road and right again over a bridge into Dolrhedyn village. Then turn left, and walk up a long climbing path by the rushing Afon Cwmorthin to Cwmorthin itself. Here, there is a beautiful secluded lake, the disused Cwmorthin quarry, and derelict buildings that remind one of a once thriving slate mining community. The steep cliffs of Allt y Ceffylau ahead will discourage further exploration! You may pick up a Cwmorthin Walk leaflet at the

Snowdonia National Park Visitor Centre which shares a building with the railway booking office at Blaenau Ffestiniog.

## Walk to Rhyd-y-Sarn

Alight at Dduallt station for this pleasant ramble to a noted beauty spot. Before World War One, Dduallt had its own station master, one Gwilym Deudraeth, a famous Welsh bard who wrote of the depressing effects of working in so lonely a spot. Follow the footpath from the top end of the station as though you are going to walk along the side of Llyn Ystradau to Tanygrisiau. Instead, turn right downhill almost immediately and follow the more or less

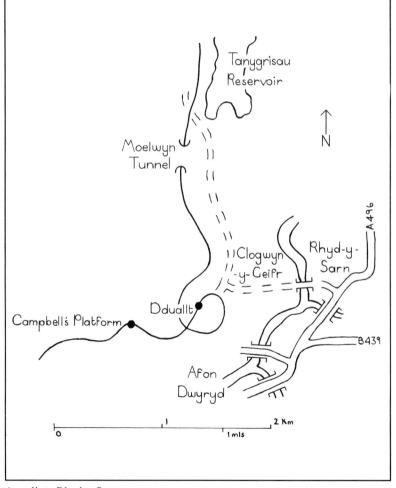

*A walk to Rhyd-y-Sarn*

straight path through the forest, by Clogwyn y Gcifr, and across the footbridge in the river gorge. Rhyd-y-Sarn lies just beyond. A sign by the path says that this walk takes one hour, but it can be done in less time if necessary.

## Walk to Llyn Mair

Alight at Tan-y-Bwlch station for this. Between the Garnedd tunnel, just over half a mile to the east of Tan-y-Bwlch station, and the station itself, there are superb views over Llyn Mair, one of the most lovely of the lakes in this spectacularly beautiful area. To reach the lake, take the clearly marked nature trail that starts at the station car park. This trail leads down to the B4410 Rhyd to Maentwrog road. This skirts part of Llyn Mair. When the road bends sharply to the right at the end of the lake, it is possible to explore, instead, the smaller path that leads, more or less straight ahead, into the woods.

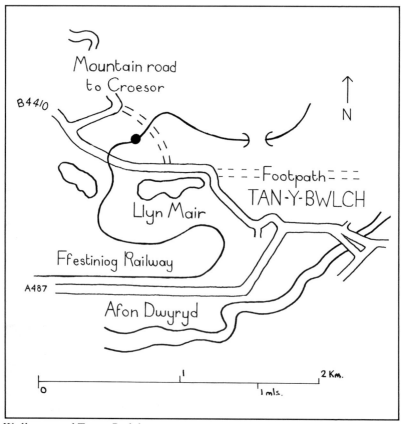

*Walks around Tan-y-Bwlch*

*Llyn Mair, easily reached from Tan-y-Bwlch station. (Ray Hill)*

*Passenger information at Tan-y-Bwlch station*

Alternatively, here you can join the walks along the well maintained footpaths in the woodlands that belong to Plas Tan-y-Bwlch, the Snowdonia National Park's magnificent Study Centre.

For a longer walk from Tan-y-Bwlch, towards the village of Croesor, turn right on top of the station footbridge and join and then follow (to the right) the mountain road. There are splendid views from Ogof Llechwyn and other places along this road. Turn back before you become too tired to enjoy further walking.

## Walk to Rhiw Goch

Alight at the Ffestiniog Railway station at Penrhyn. Join the road by the exit at the top of the station. Turn right immediately beyond the level crossing and take the farm road. At Rhiw Goch (Red Bank), approximately one mile from Penrhyn station, the road becomes a forest track. For a short circular walk, fork right past the farmhouse, cross the railway line and continue down to the main road (A487). Turn right here, and return to Penrhyn. In the centre of the town, turn right again to reach the Ffestiniog Railway station.

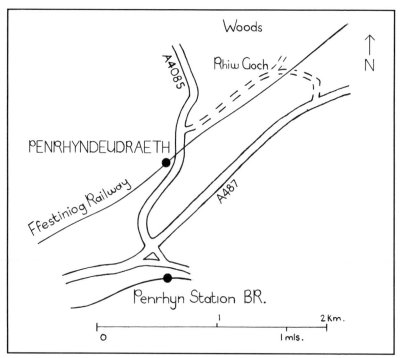

*A walk to Rhiw Goch*

## Walk to Portmeirion

It is possible to alight at Minffordd for a walk of about 1 $^1/_2$ miles long to this famous village, designed in the Italianate style by Clough Williams-Ellis. (There is a small charge for admission). It is not a particularly inspiring route, though, and many car-free visitors to Portmeirion prefer to take a Bws Gwynedd bus from Porthmadog.

The Ffestiniog Railway's terminus at Porthmadog is called The Harbour station. It offers the interesting Ffestiniog Railway Museum. Close to it is the Marine Museum which contains many exhibits illustrating the work done in the harbour in earlier decades.

On the north side of the town, on the A487 Porthmadog to Tremadoc road, close to British Rail's Cambrian Coast line Porthmadog station, you will find the coastal terminus of the Welsh Highland Railway. This charming little line is described in the next chapter.

*Attractive Portmeirion is, not surprisingly, a popular destination for visitors*

# The Welsh Highland Railway

## 9

D W Allan

*Russell and train on Gelert Farm curve*

If ever a railway was built on dreams, that line was the Welsh Highland. Its history is as complicated as the line today is short. This is only a brief summary.

The line may be said to have been born in 1872, when the success of the Ffestiniog and Talyllyn encouraged a number of "quarry owners, landed proprietors and other gentlemen" to put forward a grandiose scheme for an intricate network of narrow gauge lines that would reach most parts of Snowdonia. Their company was to be called The North Wales Narrow Gauge Railways. Little came of these amateurs' over-ambitious plans except a short 1ft 11$^1/_2$ in gauge line that started at Dinas, on the London and

North Western Railway's Caernarfon to Afon Wen line, and finished at Rhyd Ddu, three miles short of Beddgelert.

The construction even of this limited stretch had nightmare qualities. Serious difficulties arose with the contractor. As a result, no trains could run on the line until 1877. By that time, some of the ironwork on the bridges had already started to corrode.

After a relatively good year in 1878, when there were 47,000 third class passengers — most of them slate workers — the line ran quickly into more difficulties. In the following year, there was a slump in the slate trade. The number of passengers halved, and there were numerous derailments. One of the most extraordinary accidents happened when the two rear coaches of a train were left behind at the Snowdon Ranger, the station close to Llyn Cwellyn. The engine driver reversed for nearly half a mile to retrieve them, but he gave them such a bang that they were thrown on to their side. At the enquiry that followed, it came out that the driver, the fireman and the guard had all been taking liquid refreshment at the Snowdon Ranger Hotel. The guard was intoxicated, but he was "not so drunk as the driver".

Shortly after the end of World War One, the partially defunct North Wales Narrow Gauge Railways amalgamated with the Port Madoc, Beddgelert and South Snowdon Railway. This line, based on

*The road and old trackbed run side by side at the highest point of the line — 600 ft above sea level — between Beddgelert and Rhyd Ddu. (D W Allan)*

the horse-worked tramway that had carried slates from the Croesor Valley to the Quays at Port Madoc, was not much healthier. Together, the two ailing lines were to be known as The Welsh Highland Railway. Their combined routes would pass through some spectacular mountain scenery with tunnels and rock cuttings and, it was hoped, would attract tourists by the thousand. That was another dream that went wrong. In December 1924, all passenger services were suspended except those that ran in the height of summer. Even the summer services had to be discontinued in 1936. By 1942, the Welsh Highland Railway was largely dismantled. Its metal had been taken, as scrap, for the war effort.

In 1961 a group of railway enthusiasts formed a society dedicated to the memory of the Welsh Highland Railway. The society had no tangible assets: the line had been closed for 40 years; the abandoned trackbed was in the hands of the Official Receiver; there were no rails, no stock, no locomotives and no money. There was plenty of enthusiasm though — and dreams! By 1964, the society had become a company dedicated to the revival of the line.

In 1976 this dedication led to the purchase from British Rail of the old slate exchange siding at Porthmadog known as Beddgelert Sidings. This ran close to the original trackbed of the old Welsh Highland Railway and would give direct access to it when the time came. A year or so later, the company purchased Gelert's Farm, which had been built in the triangle between the old trackbed, Beddgelert Sidings, and BR's Cambrian Coast main line. This was to be the operational centre of the revived Welsh Highland Railway. Track was laid, locomotives were brought, and coaches constructed. By 1980 the Welsh Highland was back in business as a passenger-carrying railway.

During the first years of the regenerated line, trains have been able to run only as far as a temporary terminus at Pen y Mount, which is less than a mile from the Welsh Highland's terminus in Porthmadog. The enterprise has been kept going, with distinction, through the efforts of a handful of dedicated amateurs who, in true narrow gauge railway fashion, have given up much of their well-earned spare time to carry out the tasks necessary for the maintenance and provision of an adequate service on this leisurely and charming little line. Plans have been made for the extension of the railway, initially by 1 $^1/_2$ miles, to the beautiful river crossing at Pont Croesor. The possibility of the re-construction of the line to Beddgelert and perhaps even further has been discussed.

Agreements have been made for the Gwynedd County Council to buy the 22 miles long track from the Official Receiver for a nominal sum, so that it can then be leased, at a peppercorn rent, to

*Dolwyddelan Castle looking east*

*(Cadw: Welch Historic Monuments. Crown Copyright)*

*Conwy Castle from the north east*

the Welsh Highland Railway. But, all is not straightforward. Attempts have been made to lift the original firm out of liquidation by the Ffestiniog Railway, who wish to take over the restoration of the line from the Welsh Highland. The case has been considered in court. The *status quo ante* remains.

# Suggested walks

## Walk to the Aberglaslyn Pass

The old Welsh Highland Railway trackbed beyond Pen-y-Mount makes an excellent route for walkers. The gradients are easy, and the ground is well drained.

*Bryn-y-Felin bridge at the northern end of the Aberglaslyn Pass*

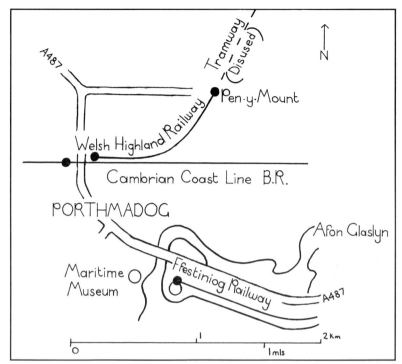

*The railway stations in Porthmadog*

The most spectacular scenery to be seen from the old trackbed is north of Nantmor, but as this village is approximately four miles away from the terminus at Pen-y-Mount this is not just an easy stroll. If you have stamina to attempt it, walk through the 300 yards long curved tunnel beyond Nantmor and enter the beautiful Aberglaslyn Pass. Cross the river at the Bryn-y-Felin bridge, keep to the right bank, and walk to the village of Beddgelert. You can cross the river again there and walk back along the other bank to Gelert's Grave. Although much visited by sightseers, it is not now believed to be the true resting place of Prince Llywelyn's faithful hound, slain by its master when he thought that it had killed his child.

Return by way of the village, the Bryn-y-Felin bridge, and the tunnel to Nantmor.

The Glanyrafon viaduct, some miles further on, is not safe for walkers to use.

*Harlech Castle still maintains a powerful presence 700 years after it was built*

## 10

# The Cambrian Coast line

## From Porthmadog to Fairbourne

A journey from BR's Porthmadog station to Fairbourne, where the Fairbourne and Barmouth Steam Railway starts, will take you through some of the most picturesque scenes in the principality. You will be travelling on part of a line — the Cambrian Coast — that has a most interesting history. If you continue your exploration as far as Tywyn, for the start of the Talyllyn railway, you will be travel-

*Train crosses Barmouth Bridge with Cader Idris in the background, 1954. (P B Whitehouse/Colour Rail)*

ling on another part of the old Cambrian Coast.

When the great Welsh railway builder David Davies of Llandinam broke up his partnership with Thomas Savin in 1864, the principal cause of the tragic disagreement between them was Savin's determination to build a great coastal railway that would run all the way from Aberystwyth in the south to Porthdinllaen on Caernarfon Bay, in the north.

Savin had decided that there should be luxury hotels at Aberystwyth, Borth, Aberdyfi, and possibly at other resorts. The cost of building such a line would be astronomic, but Savin was convinced that the enterprise would be profitable if travellers were offered tickets that entitled them to travel by train and also stay in the railway company's seaside hotels. To David Davies, this seemed like a lunatic proposition. He took the workmen loyal to him away to help him to build the line between Newtown and Machynlleth, and he left Savin alone, to translate his dreams into reality.

By August 1862, the first part of Savin's great coastal railway — the section between Machynlleth and Aberystwyth — was complete from Machynlleth to the sand dunes of Ynyslas. There, Savin put up a row of lodging houses, only to see them sinking into the sand before they were even habitable. Autumn gales then delayed the work. Savin's 'navigators' started to drink heavily, and extra police had to be drafted in to keep them in order. He had to give up his plan to build a big bridge across the Dyfi estuary, because this proved to be impossible, for geological reasons. In spite of these setbacks, Savin managed to get the line built as far as Aberystwyth. In June 1864 the first train into the town was given a civic welcome and there was much drinking and hymn singing.

Less than two years after that, Savin was bankrupt. His crazy schemes had ruined him. The newly incorporated Cambrian Railways Company took over.

Before he failed, Savin had managed to lay a track along the steep cliffs of Llwyngwril, where the hazards were so terrible that he had to employ sailors, rather than the usual navigators, because the former had better heads for heights. From here, the Cambrian Railways Company took the line to the south bank of the Mawddach estuary.

To reach Barmouth, a viaduct nearly half a mile long had to be constructed. The company used timber piles driven into the sand. Around Barmouth, the company's intentions had been ridiculed. One distinguished local resident had been so convinced of the impossibility of the enterprise that he had undertaken to eat the first locomotive that successfully crossed the estuary. At the opening of the viaduct he was taken to a table laid for one, and asked if he wanted the engine roast or boiled. The man who had dared to scoff was not amused.

From Barmouth, the company took the line to Port Madoc, and then to Pwllheli; and that was as far as it was to go. The line soon became widely renowned for its scenic grandeur. Many rail enthusiasts, today, would gladly spend much of their lives travelling from Aberystwyth to Pwllheli, and back again. Thomas Savin would have understood.

# Suggested walks

## Walk to Harlech Castle

Alight at Harlech station. The road from the station to the castle's lower entrance is steep, but from it there are good views of the attractive little town, of the Royal St David's golf course, and of the sea, bordered by distant mountains.

The castle is a remarkably complete and well-preserved example of Edward I's favourite system of concentric fortification. It was built between 1283 and 1290. The site was right by the sea, and the old watergate by which the castle can now be approached gave access, at that time, to the dock.

The castle was besieged by the Welsh prince, Madog ap Llywelyn, in 1294-5, but the garrison of 37 Englishmen managed to defend it successfully until relief came. In 1404 the castle and town were taken by Owen Glendower, who then used the place as his capital for the next four years, after which it was re-taken by the English. The castle was besieged again — this time for seven years — during the War of the Roses. It was in a bad state of repair by the time Charles I and Cromwell's forces commenced hostilities, but, even so, it was the last of the King's Welsh fortresses to fall. It was never formally slighted, but was allowed to decay gently, being of no further military use.

There is plenty to see during a walk around the castle: the great gatehouse, three storeys high, that was once used as the Constable's residence; towers and curtain walls that impress with their impenetrable strength; dungeons originally entered through trapdoors from the rooms above; and many other features at which to marvel. From the battlements, panoramic views of the mountains of Gwynedd can be enjoyed, with the Carnedd Goch group, the peaks of Snowdon itself, and the Glyders easily identifiable.

*Sheepdog demonstration at Betws y Coed*

*Midland Counties Railway 150 on the Crewe to Holyhead line near Penmaenmawr, 1989. (G W Parry/Colour Rail)*

*Snowdon Mountain Railway. (SMR)*

*Llanfair Slate Caverns*

*The formidable battlements of Harlech Castle*

## Walk to Shell Island

For this, alight at Llanbedr station. The station is about half a mile to the west of the village, on Morfa Mawr — flat land of a sort that is not uncommon on the coast of mid-Wales. On leaving the station, walk along the lane towards the sea, keeping on your left the high fences of the Royal Aerospace establishment, Llanbedr. Where the fences end, a signpost indicates the footpath, to the left, that leads to Mochras, or Shell Island. This is a peninsula that is accessible by means of a causeway, except at high tide. A small charge is made for admission. The place is noted, as its English name suggests, for the unusual quantities of shells, some of them rare, to be found on its beaches.

## A walk up the Artro Valley towards the 'Roman Steps'

This is a longer walk that also starts at Llanbedr station. This time, turn east on leaving the station and follow the road that leads to the village of Llanbedr. (There are two ancient standing stones in the fields to the left of this road.) In Llanbedr, turn left and walk for approximately 100 yards along the A496 Barmouth to Harlech road. A bridge takes this road over the little River Artro. Once across the bridge, turn right up a small road that leads in an easterly direction out of the village and up the delightful river valley.

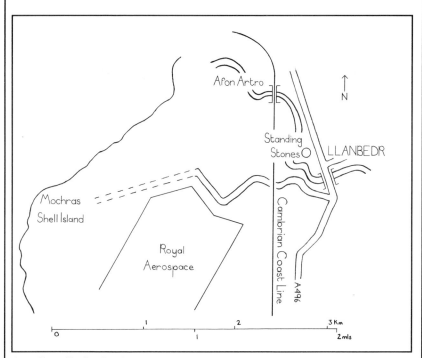

*A walk to Shell Island*

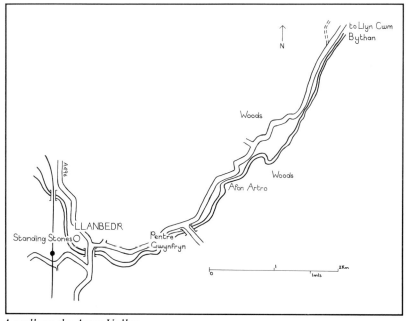

*A walk up the Artro Valley*

81

*Ffestiniog Railway at the power station summit*

*Llyn Gwynant near Beddgelert*

*Waterfall on Afon Lledr south of Betws-y-Coed*

Jim Perrin

*Ruined building in the Artro Valley*

The road can be followed for as long as you feel inclined to walk. 200 yards from the A496, the little valley road has a turning to the left. Ignore this and carry straight on. The road forks again near Pentre Gwynfryn, 1 $^1/_2$ miles from Llanbedr: take the left hand road here. There is another fork 1 $^1/_2$ miles further on: here, bear right. The lane, which keeps fairly close to the lively and beautiful little river, passes through sylvan landscapes in which, occasionally, wild goats can be glimpsed.

Eventually the lane becomes little more than a track which leads, after a long and fairly steep trudge, to Llyn Cwm Bychan, one of Snowdonia's loneliest and most impressive tarns. The track ends at Cwm Bychan farm, at the north east corner of the lake. Beyond the farm, an old pack horse trail, now a path, leads upwards to the so-called Roman Steps — rough slabs of rock forming a staircase of great antiquity.

## A walk over the Mawddach

Alight at Barmouth. The main promenade of this picturesque and popular resort makes excellent walking. So, too, does the footpath along the railway bridge that crosses the estuary. (There is a small admission charge to this path). The bridge is nearly half a mile

*Philip Evans/Countryside Commission*

*The 'Roman' Steps — probably laid in medieval times to take traffic between Bala and the Coast*

*Crib Goch with Snowdon summit emerging from cloud beyond*

*Llanberis Pass*

*Snowdon from Llyn Padarn*

Jim Perrin

*The estuary of the Mawddach at Barmouth*

long. From the path there are splendid views of the Valley of the Mawddach, with wooded hills on both sides and, in the distance, the west-facing slopes of Cader Idris. The prospect from this bridge inspired Wordsworth, visiting Barmouth in 1824, to write of the "sublime estuary".

## The Panorama walk

This starts at Barmouth, too. Access to it is by a lane that leads off the main A496 Barmouth to Tywyn road, 150 yards or so short of the Mawddach railway bridge. The path winds up and down for three miles, and is high enough above the estuary to provide some exhilarating views. At intervals there are ornate seats for walkers who would appreciate a rest.

From Morfa Mawddach station at the opposite end of the railway bridge, you may take the Morfa Mawddach walk. This beautiful and easy walk was created by the Snowdonia National Park Authority who bought the old railway trackbed between Dolgellau and Morfa Mawddach and developed it for walking and cycling.

There are several exit points along its 10 mile length, which takes in close up views of the estuary and the Cader Idris range. There are special facilities for the disabled — handrails, seats and wheelchair access — at the Morfa Mawddach end.

*Railway bridge over the Mawddach*

*Caernarfon Castle — its walls were modelled on those of Constantinople*

# The Fairbourne and Barmouth Steam Railway

## 11

*With a gauge of only 12¹/₄ in, the Fairbourne and Barmouth is the smallest of the Welsh railways*

Trains on BR's Cambrian Coast stop at Fairbourne. Many rail enthusiasts alight here so that they can enjoy travelling on the Fairbourne and Barmouth Steam Railway. This runs for two miles only, between the trim little town of Fairbourne and Porth Penrhyn, which is on a small peninsula set in the wide sands on the south bank of the Mawddach. Services connect at Porth Penrhyn with a ferry that will take passengers over the estuary to Barmouth. It is this that gives this unusual line its name. The line is unusual in another respect, too: its gauge, 12¹/₄in, makes it truly the smallest railway in Wales.

The line is now more than a century old. It was brought into existence in 1890 as a 2ft 0in gauge horse-drawn tramway. Then, the sole purpose of the line was to carry building materials from a brickyard near the site of Barmouth ferry station to the developing resort on the south bank of the Mawddach. It was owned for a time by Sir Arthur McDougall, prominent member of the family principally noted for marketing self-raising flour.

The tramway was soon opened for passenger traffic. Business increased after Fairbourne main line station was opened in 1899.

By the outbreak of World War One, land round Fairbourne had risen rapidly in value as the attractions of the little resort had become more widely known. In 1916 the tramway was bought by Narrow Gauge Railways Ltd., which was associated with the model engineering firm Bassett-Lowke of Northampton. The purchasers narrowed the gauge and introduced steam traction. Their first locomotive, the 4-4-2 tender engine *Prince Edward of Wales*, had 18in driving wheels and weighed approximately two tons.

In 1924, the line was taken over by the Fairbourne Estate and Development Company, and continued to attract holiday makers during each season. It was closed completely during World War Two, and suffered serious damage during military exercises. By Easter 1947, much of the line was ready to be brought back into use. The layout had been improved, and the signalling was being modernised. Better locomotives were bought during the 1960s, and between 1969 and 1978 an average of more than 90,000 people travelled on the line in each year.

By 1983, the railway was dilapidated. At that point, it was bought by the pop musician John Ellerton. Mr Ellerton, singer and keyboard player with the group Lynx, then divided his time between the railway and his musical career. He invested approximately £1 million in the railway and fostered the production of replicas of famous, but defunct, narrow gauge locomotives. In 1987, the railway, with its Fairbourne terminus built in the Victorian style (Gorsaf Newydd), won the Prince of Wales' award for architecture. Shortly after that, it was voted The Best Railway in Wales by Ian Allan's *Railway World* magazine.

*The award-winning Fairbourne station fully rebuilt*

*View from Porth Penrhyn station*

# The Talyllyn Railway

## 12

To reach Tywyn, starting point of the delightful Talyllyn Railway, you can travel on BR's Cambrian Coast line from Barmouth or Fairbourne. (You can approach Tywyn from Machynlleth and Aberdyfi, too, of course, if you are making a journey in the opposite direction.)

*Talyllyn Railway*

*Above: Nant Gwernol on the Talyllyn Railway.*
*Left: Train crossing Dolgoch Viaduct also on the Talyllyn line.*

Tywyn is a popular resort, with extensive beaches a little way from the centre of the town. The town increased rapidly in size in the 1870's, when much of the land around was bought by John Corbett, Member of Parliament at that time for Droitwich. Several of the buildings in the town, including the Assembly Rooms, were built in an exuberant style characteristic of the late Victorian era. The grandest hotel is a period piece that has not yet, at the time of writing, been over-discovered.

The splendid terminus of the Talyllyn Railway (Tywyn Wharf) is at the south west end of the town, close to the A493 Tywyn to Aberdyfi road, and to the BR Cambrian Coast line station. Close to the Talyllyn terminus, too, is the Narrow Gauge Railway Museum. On display here, during the season, are narrow gauge locomotives, wagons, signals, and many other items rescued from destruction at the scrap merchants' hands and beautifully restored.

The Talyllyn Railway, like other narrow gauge lines further north, was brought into existence to transport slate down from the mountains to the coast. In this instance, the line was intended to serve the Bryn Eglwys quarry in the mountains above Abergynolwyn, which was some six miles from Tywyn. The slates were transferred to main line trains on the Cambrian Coast route.

From the start, the Talyllyn Railway was designed for steam locomotion. The engineer responsible for the creation of the line was James Swinton Spooner, son of James Spooner who had been so successfully engaged in the construction of the Ffestiniog Railway. The gauge chosen was 2ft 3in, and it was agreed there would be a speed restriction of 15 mph. The only serious difficulty was posed by the ravine and waterfalls at Dolgoch. Spooner tackled this problem by constructing a three-span viaduct with a 52ft drop beneath it.

The two original 0-4-0 tanks engines *Talyllyn* and *Dolgoch* were built by Fletcher Jennings & Co. of Whitehaven. When the service started in 1866, there were two trains a day in each direction. It was the first narrow gauge railway in the world to carry both passengers and goods.

Tourists heading for Talyllyn Lake and Cader Idris were welcomed, but they were not made very comfortable, for the carriages had no lighting or heating, and smoking was not allowed. Each Monday morning at 6 o'clock a special train would leave Tywyn, taking quarrymen up to their workplace above Abergynolwyn. A primitive hostel called *The Barracks* was provided to accommodate the workers until their return to the coast on the following Friday evening.

By some extraordinary — many would say almost miraculous —

chance, the Talyllyn Railway has been in operation every year since it opened. This constitutes a world record for narrow gauge lines. It has had its share of crises however. During the economically difficult 1930's and early 1940's, the line survived only because its owner, Sir Haydn Jones, was prepared to lose money to keep it going. During World War Two, a skeleton service was operated.

By 1945 the original Fletcher Jennings locomotives were still in business, but were badly in need of overhaul and regeneration. Sir Haydn was not prepared to spend money on both, only on *Dolgoch*. In 1947, the slate quarry at the upper end of the line closed, which did not help. In the summer of 1950, Sir Haydn died, having declared that he would continue to run the trains in summer as long

*Sir Haydn heading towards Brynglas*

*Taking water at Dolgoch*

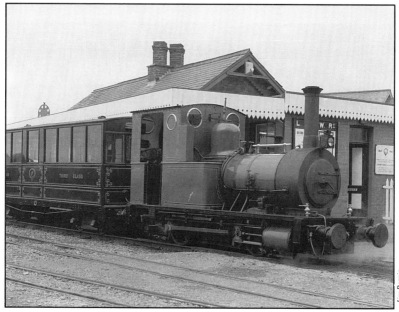

*Dolgoch, pride of the Talyllyn Railway*

as he lived. The manager, Edward Thomas, who was also the station master, guard, seller of tickets and accountant, then declared that it was extremely unlikely that the line would be able to function in the following year.

That brought the author and railway expert L T C Rolt and some of his friends into the centre of the Talyllyn Railway limelight. Quickly they formed a committee and organised the Talyllyn Railway Preservation Society. The members' aims were to raise funds to repair the track and to put the locomotives and rolling stock into good running order, using volunteer labour whenever possible.

There was much to do. The track had to be relaid. *Dolgoch*, by itself, could not provide an adequate service. Fortune, however, favoured Rolt and his friends. They were able to buy from some scrap merchants part of the track of the Corris narrow gauge railway, which had been in operation north of the River Dyfi until 1948. They found, too, and managed to purchase, a couple of the Corris 0-4-2 saddle tank engines, which had been left to decay. These were taken to Tywyn, renovated, and put into the Society's service as *Sir Haydn* and *Edward Thomas*. By the first Monday in June 1951, delighted passengers were being transported along the whole length of the line from Tywyn to Abergynolwyn and back.

# Suggested walks

## To Dolgoch ravine and waterfalls

Dolgoch station occupies a charming situation on the south east side of the mellow Fathew Valley. From the station's single platform, a footpath leads over the line by a footbridge. From this bridge there is a good view across Spooner's celebrated viaduct. The path then leads along the side of the well-wooded ravine direct to the Lower Dolgoch Falls where dippers, grey wagtails and other uncommon birds can often be observed. From the approach to these falls there is a well-maintained and clearly marked path, leading upwards. This allows a complete tour of the Dolgoch Estate with views of the other two magnificent cascades — the Middle and Upper Falls — by which the little river descends from the mountainside to the meadows below. The falls are particularly

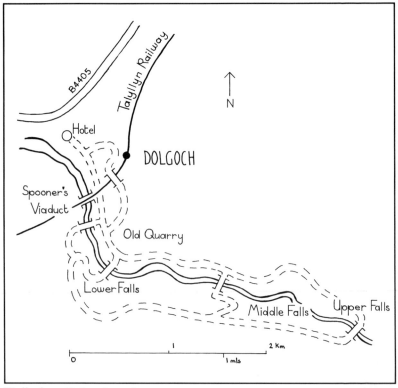

*Walks from Dolgoch station*

impressive in rainy weather, when the water thunders down in full spate.

The path returns round the boundary of the estate to Dolgoch station, so there is no need to retrace your steps. Allow at least an hour for this walk, and, preferably, if you enjoy loitering in outstandingly beautiful places, a little longer.

## A walk to Pont Cedris

Alight at Abergynolwyn for this relatively short walk which takes about an hour.

Outside the station, turn right. The B4405 leads up to the village which has shops, cafes and a most interesting quarry museum. To continue the walk, turn to the left off the B4405 and walk from the Pandy Square by way of Llanegryn Street to the bridge over the little River Dysynni. The bridge (Pont Cwrt) leads into the Cwrt. The Cwrt was at one time a more important hamlet than the Pandy, which you are just leaving.

Over the bridge, there is an iron gate on the right. Go through this, and follow the path over two stiles and up some steps to the road that leads up to the Dysynni Valley and away from Abergynolwyn.

About a mile from the village, just past Cedris

*Jim Perrin*

*Falls close to Dolgoch Station*

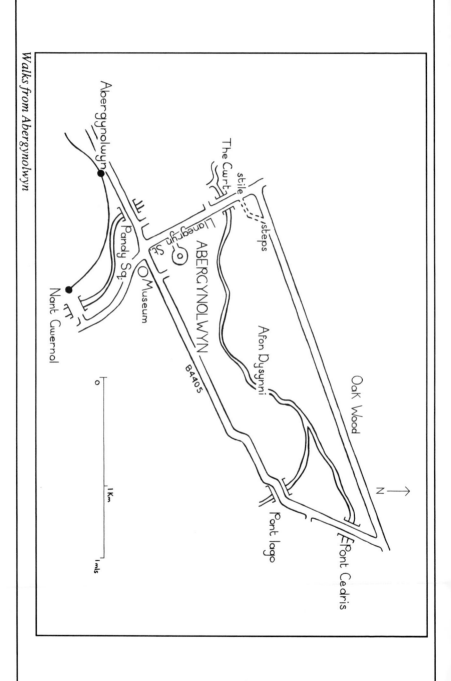

*Walks from Abergynolwyn*

Farm, the road you are on joins the B4405. Turn right here and follow the road over two bridges: first, the Pont Cedris, and then the Pont Iago, notable for the mason's mark and date, which are still visible. After the second bridge, the road leads back, past ancient oak woods and part of the Dyfi forest, to Abergynolwyn.

There are several other pleasant walks that can be made from the Talyllyn Railway's stations at Abergynolwyn and at Nant Gwernol, the railway's upper terminus. Descriptive leaflets, with maps, can be obtained at the Tywyn terminus or by post from the Conservator, Forestry Commission, Victoria House, Aberystwyth, Dyfed, SY23 2DQ. Or from the National Park's Visitor Centres or main office at Penrhyndeudraeth.

*Narrow gauge railway museum, Tywyn*

## 13

# The Bala Lake Railway

## Rheilffordd Llyn Tegid

The Bala Lake Railway is more properly known as Rheilffordd Llyn Tegid because it was the first of the restored narrow gauge railways to be incorporated in the Welsh language. This entrancing little line is rather a long way from any of British Rail's main line stations. To reach the headquarters and starting (and finishing) point of the line at Llanuwchllyn, near the south western extremity of Bala Lake, you can use the Bws Gwynedd bus service 94 that runs between Barmouth and Wrexham. The neat little railway station is reached by way of an unobtrusive approach lane entered from the B4401 road that runs through the centre of the village.

Bala Lake, or Llyn Tegid, is the largest natural lake in Wales, $3\frac{3}{4}$ miles long by, roughly, half a mile across. Several small rivers and streams flow into it. One of them, the Dyfrdwy or Little Dee, is

R Newling-Goode

believed locally to flow right through the lake without mingling its waters with those provided by less distinguished tributaries. Certainly, the lake contains a type of fish — the gwyniad — not found anywhere else in Wales. Rather less certainly, it is said also to contain a sunken town and the body of Charles the Harpist who, in the 18th century, is reputed to have given himself to the Devil by feeding communion bread to dogs. When, late one night, Charles fell into the lake and was drowned, a cloud of smoke hung over the spot where he sank.

Today, the Bala Lake Railway runs over ground skirting the lake that was once occupied by part of the Great Western Railway Company's Ruabon to Barmouth line. The line was closed in 1965 as part of the so-called 'rationalisation' of British Rail. By 1971 the track had been removed. Then George Barnes, a Lancashire engineer working at a local creamery, realised the potential value to tourists of a narrow gauge railway that could be installed where the standard gauge British Rail trains had run in pre-Beeching days. A public meeting was held in Bala. Barnes's proposals were supported by Tom Jones, the chairman of Merioneth County Council's finance committee, whose father had worked as an inspector for the GWR. There was general enthusiasm and a steering committee was formed. Narrow gauge track was bought and put down — the first ever to be laid on a standard gauge BR bed. Passenger services were started in 1972.

At first, the trains — which began their journeys at Llanuwchllyn — went only as far as Pentrepiod Crossing, very close to the side of the lake. The trains were powered by a small Ruston diesel locomotive presented to the company by Glyn Williams of Blaenau Ffestiniog. There were two open-sided bogie coaches for the paying customers — 4,300 travelled on the line in the first year.

By the following year, when 23,000 passengers were carried, a new diesel locomotive with hydraulic drive, the *Meirionydd*, built by Severn Lamb, was added. Then, in 1975, the company managed to buy from the Llanberis Lake Railway Company the steam driven Hunslet 0-4-0 tank *Maid Marian*, which had been first used in 1903 for shunting slate wagons in the Dinorwic slate quarry. With the arrival of steam, the popularity of the line increased markedly and full trains were soon being drawn along the line. This was extended through Glanllyn and Llangower to the old GWR halt, close to the town of Bala and now called Bala Lake, Bala Station, or Penybont.

The service today is charmingly informal. All trains will stop by request at the Pentrepiod, Glanllyn and Bryn Hynod halts. To join the train at these places you have to signal clearly to the driver. To alight, you have to inform the guard when you board the train. All

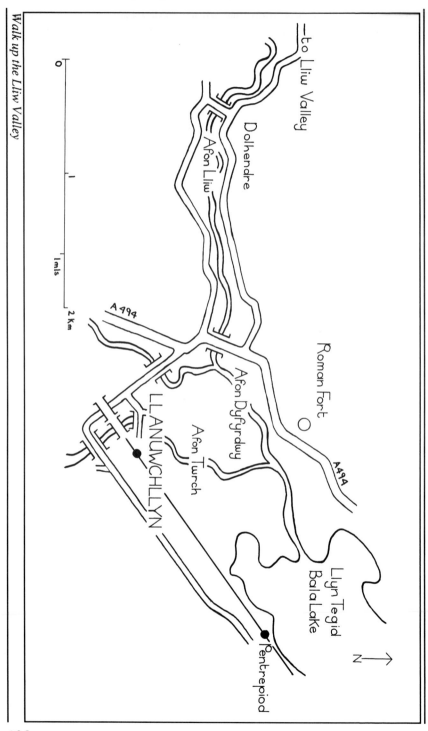

trains finish their day's work at Llanuwchllyn. It is therefore not possible to make a return trip with the last departure from Bala. It is delightful experience though to make a journey on this happy little line.

# Suggested walks

## Walk up the Lliw Valley

This is a walk that has no stated objective — to reach Trawsfynydd, as recommended in some guide books, you would need hours of difficult trudging. It would be best to enjoy the lovely scenery of this delightful valley in a leisurely way, and to turn back before you are tired.

To find the valley, leave Llanuwchllyn by the road (B4403) that forms the main street of the town and then leads in a north westerly direction towards the bridge over the River Dyfrdwy. About a quarter of a mile out of the town, it joins the A494 Barmouth to Bala Road. Turn right here, and walk as though you are aiming for Bala. Less than a quarter of a mile after you have crossed the Dyfrdwy by the road bridge you will see a lonelier road that runs off to the left and leads upwards, through the hamlets of Dolhendre and Buarthmeini, to the mountains. As you walk, look out for Castel Carndochan on the south side of the valley. This is a Norman motte on which some of the castle's foundations still survive. Further on, there are forestry plantations in which goldcrests, long tailed tits and other unusual birds may be heard and, occasionally, seen.

Of course, there are many other highly rewarding walks that can be enjoyed in the Snowdonia National Park besides those suggested in this relatively short book. Those recommended in the foregoing pages have been personally selected, from the author's experience, for their varied nature. Whatever the weather, whatever the season, they can be virtually guaranteed to provide a continuing succession of stimulating sights and sounds. And this will be true however often the walks are repeated. It is this variety that gives Snowdonia its quite unique quality as 'walking country' and for travel by train. You will find that as you explore.

# 14 | Useful information

## Information centres

**National park information centres:**
Aberdyfi (0654) 767321
Bala (0678) 520367
Betws y Coed (0690) 710665/710426
Blaenau Ffestiniog (0766) 830360
Dolgellau (0341) 422888
Harlech (0766) 780658

**National park tourist information points can be found in post offices in:**
Capel Garmon
Frongoch
Llanfachreth
Llwyngwril
Maentwrog
Mallwyd
Penmachno
Rhyd ddu
Tal y bont
Ysbyty Ifan

**National Trust Shop & information centre**
Llewelyn Cottage, Beddgelert, Gwynedd.
Tel: (076686) 293

**Wales Tourist Board information centres:**
Theatr Gwynedd, Deiniol Road, Bangor. Tel: (0248) 352786
Oriel Pendeitsh, Castle Ditch, Caernarfon. Tel: (0286) 672232
Museum of the North, Llanberis. Tel: (0286) 870765
Llanfair PG, Station Site. Tel: (0248) 713177
Porthmaadog, High Street. Tel: (0766) 512981

**Wales Tourist Board Hotline**
(0792) 645555

# General

**Cadw: Welsh Historic Monuments**
Brunel House, 2 Fitzalan Road,
Cardiff, CF2 1UY.
Tel: (0222) 465511

**Coed y Brenin Forest Park**
Aran Road, Dolgellau, Gwynedd.
Tel: (0341) 422289

**Countryside Council for Wales**
Plas Penrhos, Ffordd Penrhos, Bangor, Gwynedd, LL57 2LQ.
Tel: (0248) 370444

**Forest Enterprise**
Gwydyr Uchaf, Llanrwst, Gwynedd LL26 0PN.

**Gwynedd County Council**
County Offices,
Caernarfon, Gwynedd, LL55 1SH.
Tel: (0286) 672255

**Snowdonia National Park Authority**
National Park Office, Penrhyndeudraeth,
Gwynedd, LL48 6LS.
Tel: (0766) 770274

**National Trust**
Trinity Square, Llandudno, Gwynedd, LL30 2DE.
Tel: (0492) 74421

**Youth Hostels Association**
(Regional Office for Wales)
1 Cathedral Road, Cardiff,
CF1 9HA.
Tel: (0222) 396766

*Youth Hostels at:*
Bala (0678) 520215
Bangor (0248) 353516
Bryn Gwynant (076686) 251
Capel Curig (06904) 225
Idwal Cottage  (0248) 600225
Kings (Dolgellau) (0341) 422392
Llanbedr (Harlech) (034123) 287
Llanberis (0286) 870280
Lledr Valley (06906) 202
Penmaenmawr (0492) 623476
Pen y Pass (0286) 870428
Roewen (0222) 396766
Snowdon Ranger (028685) 391

# Travel

*Leaflets, timetables and further information from information centres above or by post from:*
The County Planning Officer
**Gwynedd County Council,**
County Offices, Caernarfon,
Gwynedd, LL55 1SH.
Tel: (0286) 679378

# Railways

*For enquiries re* **Crewe to Holyhead, Conwy Valley and Cambrian Coast lines***:* Tel: British Rail enquiries

**Bala Lake Railway**
The Station,
Llanuwchllyn, Bala,
Gwynedd, LL23  7DD.
Tel: (06784) 666

**Fairbourne & Barmouth Steam Railway**
Beach Road, Fairbourne,
Gwynedd, LL38 2PZ.
Tel: (0341) 250362

**Ffestiniog Railway**
Harbour Station,
Porthmadog, Gwynedd,
LL49 9NF.
Tel: (0766) 512340/831654

**Llanberis Lake Railway**
Gilfach Ddu, Llanberis,
Caernarfon, Gwynedd,
LL55 4TY.
Tel: (0286) 870549

**Snowdon Mountain Railway**
Llanberis, Caernarfon,
Gwynedd.
Tel: (0286) 870223

**Talyllyn Railway**
Wharf Station, Tywyn,
Gwynedd, LL36 9EY.
Tel: (0654) 710472

**Welsh Highland Railway**
Gelerts Farm Works, Madoc
Street West,
Porthmadog, Gwynedd.

*Nant Gwernol station on the Talyllyn Railway*

# Castles/Historic buildings

### Bangor Cathedral
*Founded circa 525 but destroyed several times until its restoration in the late 15th, early 16th and 19th centuries.*
Tel: (0248) 354204

### Bryn Bras Castle & Gardens
*Neo-Romantic castle set in 32 acres. Walled Knot garden, tea room and tea garden, picnic area. Open daily (except Saturdays) spring bank holiday to end of September.*
Llanrug, Nr Caernarfon,
Gwynedd.
Tel: (0286) 870210

### Beaumaris Castle
*World Heritage "site of outstanding value". Example of concentric castle. Commands superb views of Menai Straits*
Tel: (0248) 810361

### Caernarfon Castle
*World Heritage "site of outstanding value". Unique angular walls and towers. Three exhibitions, Royal Welch Fusiliers Regimental Museum, gift shop and guided tours.*
Tel: (0286) 77617

### Cochwillan Hall & Mill
Tal y bont, Bangor, Gwynedd.
Tel: (0248) 364608 *(Hall)* 362800 *(Mill)*

### Conwy Castle
*World Heritage "site of outstanding value". Masterpiece of medieval architecture built during reign of Edward I. Also information centre and exhibition.*
Tel: (0492) 592358

## Criccieth Castle

*Established circa 1230 by Llywelyn the Great; features high twin-towered gatehouse. Two award-winning exhibitions.*
Tel: (0766) 522227

## Dolbadarn Castle

*Built by Llwellyn the Great circa 1200.*
Llanberis (no phone)

*Part of Gwydir Castle, Llanrwst*

**Dolwyddelan Castle**
*Built by Welsh princes in 13th Century. Exhibition located in the keep.*
Tel: (0690) 6366

**Gwydir Castle**
*A fine country house set in beautiful gardens.*
Llanrwst
Tel: (0492) 641687

**Gwydir Uchaf Chapel**
*Built in 1673; noted for its 17th century painted ceiling.*
Tel: (0492) 640978

**Harlech Castle**
*World Heritage "site of outstanding value". Built between 1283 and 1289 by Edward I, it was later captured by Owain Glyndwr. Represents high point in medieval castle construction. Exhibition.*
Tel: (0766) 780552

**Penrhyn Castle**
*Early 19th century Neo Norman fantasy castle by Thomas Hopper. Contains important collection of old masters, a doll museum and an industrial railway museum.*
Nr. Bangor, Gwynedd.
Tel: (0248) 353084

**Plas Newydd**
*Elegant 18th century house built by James Wyatt. Rex Whistler exhibition, military museum with relics of the Battle of Waterloo. Rhododendron garden in spring.*
Llanfairpwll, Anglesey.
Tel: (0248) 714795

**Segontium**
*Remains of Roman fort. Exhibition of Roman life presented by the National Museum of Wales.*
Nr. Caernarfon, Gwynedd.
Tel: (0286) 5625

**Ty Mawr**
*Birthplace of Bishop William Morgan (1545-1604), first translator of the Bible into Welsh. Display of Welsh bibles.*
Wybrnant, Nr Penmachno, Gwynedd.
Tel: (06903) 213

# Museums/Centres

**Caernarfon Air Museum**
*Planes, helicopters, over 200 model aircraft, cinema, displays, aviation history. Adventure playground.*
Caernarfon Airport, Dinas Dinlle, Caernarfon.
Tel: 0286 830800/831047

**Centre for Alternative Technology**
*See page 119*
Machynlleth, Powys.
Tel: 0654 702400

**Conwy Valley Railway Museum**
The Old Goods Yard, Betws y Coed, Gwynedd.
Tel: (0690) 710568

**Glynllifon Heritage Park**
*Historic gardens and woodland, environmental sculpture, 18th century fort, 19th century hermitage, restored estate workshops, tearooms.*
Llandwrog.
Tel: (0286) 830222

**Industrial Locomotive Museum**
Penrhyn Castle, Bangor, Gwynedd.
Tel: (0248) 353084

In an attractive wooded valley north of Machynlleth, on the site of a reclaimed quarry, can be found the renewable energy movement's British shrine — the Centre for Alternative Technology.

For 17 years — since it was set up by the philanthropic industrialist Gerard Morgan-Grenville, in response to his concern over the energy crisis — the Centre has been practising what it preaches.

On arrival, visitors cross a line, beyond which, they are told, there is no mains electricity supply. A walk up into the former quarry basin reveals a thriving community, self-sufficient and employing up to 40 people, whose displays, exhibits, shop and restaurant were visited by a remarkable 75,000 people in 1990.

The Centre offers advice to people wanting to make use of alternative technologies and is a working model of what can be achieved, from sewage sludge digester plants and organic gardens, to solar panels and wind turbines.

The Centre enjoys a significant local reputation and has spawned three outside businesses.

Machynlleth can be reached by rail on either the Central Wales or Cambrian Coast line. From there you can walk, cycle or catch a bus to the centre which is open seven days a week and offers a full restaurant service from March to the end of October. For further information telephone 0654 702400

## Inigo Jones (slate works)

*Established 1861. Perhaps last surviving example of a fully operational slate works in North Wales. Craftsmen at work, audio visual presentation, cafe. Facilities for disabled.*
Groeslon, Gwynedd.
Tel: (0286) 830242

## Llanfair Slate Caverns

*Guided tours to old workings along tunnels and caverns. Refreshments and crafts shop. Open Easter to mid-October including Sundays.*
Nr Harlech.
Tel: (0766) 780247

## LLechwedd Slate Caverns

*Underground tramway and Deep mine with chambers and tunnels. Victorian village on the surface with exhibitions, gifts, craft shop, pub, working smithy, cafe and restaurant. Open all year.*
Blaenau Ffestiniog, Gwynedd.
Tel: (0766) 830306

## Lloyd George Memorial Museum & Highgate

*Boyhood home of the famous statesman recreated as it would have been when he lived there. Plus his Uncle Lloyd's shoemaker's workshop, "talking head" displays, audio-visual theatre, Victorian schoolroom and library.*
Llanystumdwy, Criccieth, Dwyfor.
Tel: (0766) 522071

## Maes Artro Village

*Wartime RAF camp turned visitor centre with museum, sea life aquarium, village of yesteryear, garden centre, craft shops and exhibitions.*
Llanbedr, Gwynedd.
Tel: (0341 23) 467

*Snowdonia's National Park Study Centre (Plas Tan y Bwlch), situated one mile west of Maentwrog, offers courses for anyone interested in the countryside. Set in magnificent grounds — which are home to many old and rare trees — it was established in 1975 and has accommodation for 54 people.*

*The centre plays an important role in the local community whose members can draw up a programme of activities in consultation with staff. There is also an increasing number of courses in the Welsh language and an environmental education programme for young people.*

*Most courses are taught by permanent staff, although the centre also attracts outside lecturers.*

*Among recent developments is a wide variety of professional courses, sponsored by the Countryside Council for Wales, to provide professional training for countryside staff from both England and Wales.*

*The centre also often plays host to important regional conferences and seminars and welcomes groups from abroad.*

*The centre can be reached by British Rail (except on Sundays) to Blaenau Ffestiniog (via Llandudno Junction) or Penrhyndeudraeth for connection with local buses. Further information is available from the centre, telephone (076 685) 324.*

## Motor Museum
*Vintage and post vintage cars including Bugatti type 57, Riley MPH, Aston Martin, MGs, Rolls Royce, Austin 7, Morris Cowley, Alvis and Ford.*
Betws y Coed.
Tel: (06902) 632/427

## Museum of Memories
*Historical costumes, lace collection, embroideries, taped introduction.*
Jenny Jones museum and gift shop,
Betws y Coed, Gwynedd.

## Museum of the North
*Power of Wales exhibition. Tour of Dinorwig power station shows how electricity is generated from water.*
Amgueddfa'r, Gogledd, Llanberis, Gwynedd.
Tel: (0286) 870636/871331

## National Centre for Mountain Activities
(Plas y Brenin)
*Canoeing, abseiling and dry slope skiing during July and August. Visitor information. Food available in bar with views of Snowdon Horseshoe.*
Capel Curig, Betws y Coed, Gwynedd.

## National Watersports Centre
Llanfairisgaer, Caernarfon, Gwynedd.
Tel: (0248) 670964

**Quarry Hospital Museum**
Padarn Country Park, Llanberis. *See below*

**RSPB Wild Snowdonia**
*RSPB information centre, sounds and visual effects, computer games, children's play area. Free admission.*
Y Stablau, Betws y Coed, Gwynedd.
Tel: (0492) 710768

**Segontium Roman Fort Museum**
Ffordd Llanbeblig, Caernarfon.
Tel: (0286) 5625

**Snowdonia National Park Exhibition**
Y Stablau Visitor Centre,
Betws y Coed, Gwynedd.
Tel: (0690) 710665

**Snowdonia National Park Study Centre**
(Plas Tan y Bwlch)
*(See page 121)*
Maentwrog, Blaenau Ffestiniog, Gwynedd.
Tel: (0766 85) 324/334

**Sygun Copper Mine**
*19th century mine with tunnels, chambers and stalactite and stalagmite formations. Visitor centre and guided tours.*
Beddgelert, Caernarfon, Gwynedd.
Tel: (0766 86) 595

**Trefriw Woollen Mills**
*Weaving displays, hydro-electric turbines. Shop & cafe.*
Trefriw, Gwynedd.
Tel: (0492) 640462

**Welsh Quaker Exhibition**
*Exhibition and video depicting the history of Quakerism in Meirionnydd area.*
Ty Meirion, Snowdonia National Park Visitor Centre,
Dolgellau, Gwynedd.
Tel: (0341) 422888

**Welsh Slate Centre**
*Workshop complex built in 1870; original equipment on display.*
*Regular demonstrations.*
Y Gilfach Ddu, Llanberis.
Tel: (0286) 870630

## Other places of interest

**Aber Falls**
Spinneys Nature Reserve, Aber

**Bangor Pier**
*Restored, award winning Victorian pier with shops, restaurant,*
*cafe and amusements.*
Ffordd Gwynedd, Bangor, Gwynedd.
Tel: (0248) 352421

**Bodnant Garden**
*Nearly 100 acres of garden situated in the Conwy Valley. Open*
*every day mid-March to end of October. Refreshment pavilion.*
*Plants, books and gifts for sale.*
Tal y Cafn, Colwyn Bay.
Tel: (0492) 650460

*On the Llanberis Lake Railway in the Padarn Country Park*

**Padarn Country Park**
*Lake railway, watersports centre, craft workshops, slate museum, walks, quarryman's hospital, shops, tea rooms.*
Llanberis. Tel: (0286) 870892

**Portmeirion**
*Setting for cult TV series "The Prisoner" — Italianate village on wooded peninsula overlooking Cardigan Bay. Shops, hotel, audio visual show, woods, gardens and beaches. Open all year.*
Nr Porthmadog, Gwynedd.
Tel: (0766) 770228

## Swimming pools/Leisure centres

Bangor (0248) 370600
Caernarfon (0286) 76451
Harlech (0766) 780576
Llanberis (0286) 870993
Llanrwst (0492) 640921
Plas Menai (0248) 670964
Tywyn (0654) 711763

## Theatres/Cinemas

Victoria, Bala (0678) 520800
Theatr Gwynedd, Bangor (0248) 351708
Octagon Entertainment Centre, Bangor (0248) 354977
Plaza Cinema, Bangor (0248) 362059
Dome Entertainment Centre, Caernarfon (0286) 76069
Coliseum, Porthmadog (0766) 512108
Theatre Ardudwy, Harlech (0766) 780667
Cinema, Tywyn (0654) 710260
Dragon Theatre, Barmouth (The Community Centre)

# RailTrail

## Books from Leading Edge

### The Isle of Man by Tram, Train and Foot — *Stan Basnett and David Freke,* £5.99

Specially revised and updated for the 1993 centenary of the Manx Electric Railway, this hugely popular volume is a must for anyone making a trip to the Island, which boasts not just the celebrated Edwardian trams of the MER, but also the Snaefell mountain line, the Victorian steam railway, the Douglas horse trams and more.

### The Great Metro Guide to Tyne and Wear — *Vernon Abbott and Roy Chapman,* £5.95

There can be no better way to explore the fascinating towns and cities beside these great rivers, and the fine coastline and countryside just minutes away by the area's excellent Metro system. "Just the ticket," *Evening Chronicle.*

### Settle & Carlisle Country — *Colin Speakman and John Morrison,* £5.95

Features the Settle-Carlisle Way, a new walkers' route from Leeds to Carlisle, inaugurated by Mike Harding, as well as a cycle route from Skipton to Carlisle. "Just what we needed," wrote Michael Leapman in his report on an S & C walking holiday, in *The Independent.*

### Pennine Rails and Trails — *John Morrison and Lydia Speakman,* £5.75

Like *Settle & Carlisle Country*, this book on the South Pennines is superbly illustrated by John Morrison's photographs. A foreword by Mike Harding commends it as the ideal way to explore his old stamping ground. "A real joy to read and study," *Lancashire Magazine.*

### Exploring Strathclyde by Rail — *Tom Noble,* £5.75

When Glasgow was designated European City of Culture in 1990, it ensured wider recognition for its superb architecture and fine museums and galleries. Armed with this book, the visitor will be ideally equipped to discover not only Glasgow, but much of the surrounding coast and countryside. "You'd be lost without it," *Evening Times.*

## DUE SPRING 1993:

### Discovering North Norfolk and the Broads — *Debbie Bartlett,* £6.99.   Hidden Places of Mann — *Stan Basnett,* £5.99

**Leading Edge, Old Chapel, Burtersett, Hawes, N. Yorks, DL8 3PB.**

*Postage and packing charges — orders over £2, add 75p; over £6, add £1.*

## ☎ (0969) 667566

# Railway and transport books

*from Leading Edge*

### The Great Railway Conspiracy

*Few books on railways in recent years have stirred so much controversy and wide interest as David Henshaw's extraordinary account of the Beeching Years which touches many raw nerves in road haulage, and broader political circles. "Henshaw tells the tale well and uncovers much skulduggery," The Daily Mail. £7.95, paperback, £14.95, hardback.*

### Traffic Congestion: Is there a way out?

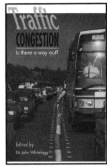

*A remarkable collection of papers which blows apart surviving myths about road-building as a solution to congestion. Edited by leading public authority, Dr John Whitelegg. "The expert contributors advance some radical solutions to the dead-end street that the road lobby is forcing us down," Transport Review.*
£9.95, paperback

### The Wensleydale Railway

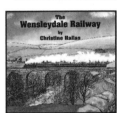

*Christine Hallas tells, in remarkable detail, the story of an English country railway, whose future is now topical, as the subject of ambitious reinstatement plans. "A splendid publication and good value for money," Push and Pull magazine.*
£5.25, paperback

### The Line that Refused to Die

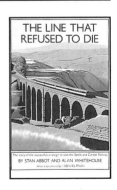

*In this revised and updated version of their best-seller, Stan Abbott and Alan Whitehouse tell the story of the successful campaign to save the Settle & Carlisle line -- and add some words on the ongoing story of this and Britain's other rural railways. Features a foreword by Michael Palin. "The authors have a remarkable story to tell, of intrigue in high places, of U-turns, of hopes dashed and deferred, of leaks and nods and whispers and labyrinthine negotiations," The Yorkshire Post. £7.99, paperback.*

**Leading Edge, Old Chapel, Burtersett, Hawes, N. Yorks, DL8 3PB.**

*Postage and packing charges — orders over £2, add 75p; over £6, add £1.*

# ☎ (0969) 667566

## You've read the book, you've done the walks... Now, wear the T-shirt and drink from the mug...

**RailTrail** *T-shirts and mugs available now by mail order from Leading Edge*

❖ T-shirts — 100 per cent cotton with **RailTrail** logo, as above, in full colour. Only £6 including post and packing.

❖ Mugs — full colour chunky mug with **RailTrail** logo. Just £2.95.

*Just phone us with your order, stating size of T-shirt and quoting your credit card number and expiry date. Or send cheque with order to:*

**Leading Edge (retail sales), Old Chapel, Burtersett, Hawes, North Yorks, DL8 3PB**

☎ **(0969) 667566**